APPROACHING JEHOVAH'S WITNESSES IN LOVE

[signature]

P Ml L, 2:16

APPROACHING JEHOVAH'S WITNESSES IN LOVE

HOW TO WITNESS EFFECTIVELY WITHOUT ARGUING

Wilbur Lingle

CHRISTIAN • LITERATURE • CRUSADE
Fort Washington, Pennsylvania 19034

CHRISTIAN LITERATURE CRUSADE

U.S.A.
P.O. Box 1449, Fort Washington, PA 19034

GREAT BRITAIN
51 The Dean, Alresford, Hants., SO24 9BJ

AUSTRALIA
P.O. Box 91, Pennant Hills, N.S.W. 2120

NEW ZEALAND
P.O. Box 77, Ashhurst

This Printing 1994

ISBN 0-87508-702-7

PRINTED IN THE UNITED STATES OF AMERICA

CONTENTS

FOREWORD

For many years I knew about as much as the average Christian does about the cults. That wasn't very much, and it was outdated. But then, in March 1975, something happened that completely changed the course of my ministry.

My wife, Jean, and I had gone to Japan in 1954 as missionaries. We served in a church-planting ministry there for thirty-five years, until 1989. In March 1975 we were working with our second church, Njijgaoka (Rainbow Hill) Bible Church, which we had started thirteen years earlier. We had spent much time making contacts and trying to establish a good reputation in the area. But then Mormon missionaries from the U.S. moved into the area where we had our church and began going around telling people that I was of the devil and that they should not attend my church.

Shortly after this, these men came to my church and wanted me to read the Book of Mormon and study with them. I was busy, but since they were in the area and were causing trouble, I decided to have talks with them and find out exactly what they believed. That way, if the Christians in my church were to ask me the difference between true Christianity and Mormonism, I would know. I told the Mormon fellows I would talk with them if they would keep coming back for at least two to three months—until I had sufficient time to read the entire Book of Mormon. They promised to do this.

So I began to meet with them—and quickly learned I did not know how to witness to them effectively. I hurriedly borrowed every cult book I could get my hands on. These books gave me facts, but they did not tell me how to witness. I felt frustrated and ineffective.

These first Mormon missionaries came only several times. Later, however, I got in contact with other Mormon missionaries. Gradually, with much studying and witnessing, I came to where I felt I could effectively witness to them.

About this time the Jehovah's Witnesses began to grow and become more active in Japan. Our church had a class for three-year-old children with sixty in attendance. We had a Bible class for the mothers of these children twice each month. The J.W.'s started visiting in our area. When they came to the mothers of the children in our class and found out they were attending the Bible class, they would say, "It is really wonderful that you have an interest in the Bible. We also study the Bible. I think it would be good if we could come to your home and study the Bible together." In this way they were able to deceive some of the mothers and they joined their group. It was a while before I found out what was going on and was able to warn the mothers of this danger.

Shortly after this, some J.W.'s came to my house and wanted me to study with them. I agreed to do so. In my attempt to evangelize them I used the typical approach of starting with John 1:1—the deity of Christ and the Trinity—and with the doctrine of hell. This approach, I quickly found out, wasn't very effective. I didn't feel that I was making much progress. Again I read every cult book I could find. In vain I searched for material that would enable me to witness effectively. But I did not give up. I kept witnessing to the J.W.'s every opportunity I had and continued to do a vast amount of reading. I began to find a few effective ways of witnessing but did not yet feel satisfied with the progress I was making.

Eleven years later, in the fall of 1986, I felt I made a real breakthrough. At this time I was in the States on furlough. I learned about a conference for ex-Jehovah's Witnesses that was being held for three days in the Pocono Mountains of Pennsylvania. I attended this conference and asked as many as possible how they had been saved, to see if there might be some key that I was missing. Without exception, they all told me that it was only after they began to question the Watchtower *Organization* that they no longer believed the interpretations that the Watchtower Society had put upon the Scriptures.

This was the key that I was looking for! I had been working on how to answer the interpretations—a very long and difficult assignment. I realized that I had been trying to kill the tree, so to speak, by cutting off the many branches (the individual arguments); I saw it was much better to kill the tree by cutting at the roots (showing the discrepancies within the *source* of the arguments, the organization).

After this, I began to gear my witnessing toward undermining the organization. It soon became evident that this was much more effective and less frustrating. Previously, a Jehovah's Witness ordinarily had the advantage over me because he was so well prepared . . . but now I was taking him into new and unfamiliar territory. As I continued to deal with as many J.W.'s as possible, I kept coming up with more thought-provoking questions to ask the Witnesses concerning the Watchtower Organization.

After having spent so much time and effort in my attempt to witness to the J.W.'s, I now wish to pass on the things I have learned with the hope that other Christians, who are struggling as I did, might benefit.

Every time I deal with Jehovah's Witnesses I come away with tears inside because of the sad condition of their hearts. Jehovah's Witnesses may seem to be bold, but as you talk to them you realize the emptiness that they have in their hearts. They have nothing in their religion that will fill that emptiness.

The intent of this book is to give you a burden for the Jehovah's Witnesses and adequate knowledge to be able to witness to them successfully. It can be used for individual or group study.

May I give one very important word of warning. If you are a new convert to Christianity, I strongly urge you not to attempt to witness to a Jehovah's Witness on your own. They are very well trained and will easily get you thoroughly confused. Have a mature Christian enter into the witnessing with you.

If you are a pastor, as you gain experience in witnessing to Jehovah's Witnesses by using the material in this book you can in turn train your church members to be effective witnesses. Also ask your church members to keep you informed of their meetings with Jehovah's Witnesses and of the progress that is made.

May the Lord bless you as you study to become a successful witness to the Jehovah's Witnesses. My prayer is that He will give you a burden to reach these lost souls for Christ.

Wilbur Lingle
August 1994

CHAPTER ONE

AN OVERVIEW

Many people have the impression that Jehovah's Witnesses are devout, moral people, with much zeal for their religion. Some call them good neighbors and hard-working. When they go from door to door, they are always neatly dressed, have a friendly smile, and are polite when they first meet you at your door. Most people have not had enough close contact with a Jehovah's Witness to discover what is behind the neat clothing and smile.

If I could take a picture of their hearts and put it on display, you would see a person who is carrying a heavy burden of sin and is driven by a continual fear that he will not be pleasing to Jehovah God. He is in deep bondage to the Watchtower organization. Most hate going door-to-door. If it was not for the organization's disfellowshipping policy, half would quickly leave. They are empty people and are in desperate need of help. They need to meet and come to know the Lord Jesus Christ. Born-again Christians must take time and have the patience to lovingly explain the way of salvation to them.

Many Christians shy away from talking to Jehovah's Witnesses. Some do try, but generally after half an hour to an hour of sharp conflict they give up and consider it hopeless. Some, though, persevere and manage to get the Jehovah's Witnesses to come back, but they can't get them to return more than two or three times.

How are we going to get close to these people? How can we pierce the emotional barrier? How can we deal with them long enough for them to come to the conclusion that the Watchtower organization is definitely not what it claims to be—and for them to begin to consider the claims of Christ? Is there a solution to this problem?

There are many books on the cults that will give you the basic facts, but they ordinarily do not tell you how to use these facts in witnessing. Other books will tell you how you can argue the Jehovah's Witness down. Still other books will give you a few pages on the particular cult and then say, "Just pray that the Holy Spirit will give you wisdom and then get out your Bible and go after them." But the Holy Spirit does not bless ignorance. An oversimplified approach like this is insufficient to prepare us to meet the Jehovah's Witness, who has been thoroughly indoctrinated and is well prepared to debate. In fact, this approach merely plays into their hands; they are more than ready to answer the verses most Christians use.

This is a unique book, unlike anything else available. I have not written from theory, but from eighteen years of study and personal witnessing to Jehovah's Witnesses. I have received much feedback from people who have used the approach set forth in this book. It shows how you can have meaningful, nonconfrontational encounters with a Jehovah's Witness over many weeks. It also explains how you can get him to open his heart by first building a friendship with him, and then by asking him questions to make him *think* regarding the Watchtower organization. In the process, he will begin to see that the Watchtower Society is not what it claims to be. It is an approach of *asking* him and not *telling* him; thus it will be his conclusion and not yours. This approach does not attack the individual. Rather, using the information in this book will bring one to the point where he will be willing to listen amicably to the message of salvation.

And now for a chapter-by-chapter overview of this book.

• •

When Jehovah's Witnesses are canvassing door-to-door, they usually don't want to enter into a lengthy conversation at that time; they are just making contacts so that they can return later. You can use this first meeting to your advantage. Your first few minutes with them are very important. How to utilize this initial contact and get them to promise that they will come back for a predetermined period is explained in the following chapter, Chapter Two.

• • •

Chapter Three discloses how you can present the plan of salvation by giving your personal testimony in the very first session of your scheduled appointments—while the Jehovah's Witness is still wearing his or her well-practiced smile. You must know how to present your testimony so that the Jehovah's Witness does not feel that you are preaching to him—but simply sharing with him the spiritual journey you had before you met Christ, and what happened when you believed.

• • • •

It is also important to know something of the history of the Watchtower movement. I have set this forth in Chapter Four. There are not many details, just enough so that you can understand what has taken place and be aware of some of the many changes which have occurred over the years.

• • • • •

It is often difficult to find out what Jehovah's Witnesses really believe. Their books are deceptive. If a person reads them and takes them at face value, he will be mislead. Chapter Five explains what biblical Christianity teaches in contrast to the beliefs of the Watchtower Society. I am sure you will discover some startling facts you are not likely to find in any other book. I give this material not so you can better argue doctrine but to help you to know and understand their beliefs. I have tried to make their teachings clear.

• • • • • •

Jehovah's Witnesses claim that they alone practice the true religion and that the Watchtower Society is "God's sole channel of communication to this earth." That means all other beliefs are false and of the devil. Repeatedly they teach their people that what they practice proves they are the true religion. Chapter Six is an examination of what they consider to be their twelve distinctive, authenticating practices. They will quote Matthew 7:20 which says, "By their fruits ye shall know them." You will soon discover when dealing with Jehovah's Witnesses that they are very proud of their "fruits." It is helpful to know these twelve "fruits." The analysis given will help them realize that these "fruits" are not peculiar to the Jehovah's Witnesses—and that even if they were, they still do not prove that the Watchtower way is the true religion.

• • • • • • •

The real heart of the book is in Chapter Seven. Here you will find many unsettling questions to ask a Jehovah's Witness—to cause him to think and get him to realize that the Watchtower organization is false. Jehovah's Witnesses operate on what I call a "push-button mentality." The approach Christians generally use and the objections they raise are practically standardized; Jehovah's Witnesses are well trained to "refute" these expected arguments. They have gone over them so often that they have them memorized. Thus, when a Christian uses any of these oft-repeated arguments, the Jehovah's Witness quickly proceeds to quote the memorized answer. He never thinks through the question or the answer. It has not become a part of him. If you happen to ask a question for which he doesn't have a memorized answer, he turns to the book *Reasoning from the Scriptures*, which will more than likely have the answer—which he will then read to you. Again, he does not have to think.

It is important to get Jehovah's Witnesses to think for themselves. You can do this by asking them all-new questions, found in this book—ones which they are not familiar with and for which there are no standard answers or Watchtower articles available to help them. These questions are not argumentative but only thought-provoking, so you don't have to get a "right" answer. The doubts sown by the questions are much more important than the answers. These questions will repeatedly cause the Jehovah's Witness to have to contradict himself.

I designed these questions to show that the Watchtower organization has frequently changed its teachings through the years. By the Society's own admission, they will continue to change. The Watchtower publications refer to those who join their organization as those who come into "the truth." However, they constantly have to keep *readjusting* the truth. They claim that they continually receive "new light" which eliminates the pagan and apostate teachings formerly held by their organization. They consider that this explanation justifies their many changes. Yet one has to ponder where this "new light" comes from. If it were really coming from God, then it would be eternal truth and could never change. But what they claim is "new light" and "the truth today" may be subject to change, and thus *false*, tomorrow.

Often they have come out with "new light" that is exactly opposite to what they have been teaching. But in the future they will disregard this "new light" and go back to the original teaching. Later they will present this old, disregarded teaching as "new light." They also claim that they will continue to receive "new light"—which means that they do not have the truth now, because truth can't change. Through the questions in Chapter Seven a Jehovah's Witness should come to realize, and eventually admit, that the Watchtower Society cannot be relied upon.

There is not much presented in this book that needs to be memorized. You can take the questions right from the book, so it is much easier to witness. These questions are intended to make the Jehovah's Witness explain the actions of the organization, which is difficult for them to do. They can argue on the interpretation of many Bible verses, but they are not prepared to defend the changing beliefs and false assumptions of the Watchtower organization. They often say, "At least, when we make mistakes we admit them." This is well and good, but it does not compensate for the damage their mistakes cause and does not prevent them from making more mistakes in the future. The Christian is saved by the precious blood of the Lord Jesus Christ, not by his or her good works, or any church or organization. Thus the Christian does not have to defend a church. But the Jehovah's Witness has to defend his organization because they claim that there is no salvation outside the Watchtower organization.

As you use the questions in Chapter Seven and come to recognize the type of question that causes them to *think* and to see their organization's discrepancies, you can come up with your own questions.

Let me give you an example of one set of questions. When Jehovah's Witnesses approach you, they usually point out the crime, drugs, immorality, war, evil, famine, earth-quakes, etc., in this world. They will ask if you would be interested in living in a beautiful paradise on earth. They might even show you a picture with a large house, a lush garden with all kinds of fruits and vegetables, a clear lake in the foreground and a snow-capped mountain in the back-ground. You can begin from this point.

Question #1: Your description of the new earth sounds very inviting, but I have a problem understanding how the earth and its inhabitants are transformed from this present evil condition into the beautiful, paradise-like conditions you describe. Does something just go "poof" and this "new world order" suddenly appears?

Response #1: Well, it's not exactly like that. You see, before the new world order comes forth, Armageddon must occur.

Question #2: When does Armageddon happen?

Response #2: It will happen very soon.

Question #3: What happens at Armageddon?

Response #3: Just about all this world will be destroyed.

Question #4: How is this going to occur?

Response #4: (You probably will receive a vague an-swer, but their books and magazines contain vivid pictures of massive earthquakes, the earth swallowing up people, large buildings crumbling, fires destroying cities, and floods causing people to float down rivers. They also declare that people will massacre each other, and those who do not die in these ways will be killed by God's angels.)

Question #5: Will everyone living upon this earth be killed at this time?

Response #5: Everyone but faithful Jehovah's Witnesses. (Your respondents might be vague, but this is what they believe and teach.)

Question #6: How will it be possible that only Jehovah's Witnesses survive when everyone else will be killed?

Response #6: Jehovah in some miraculous way will protect us.

Question #7: You mean that Jehovah's Witnesses will live through this horrible disaster, witnessing these people being killed, and will have to listen to the blood-curdling screams as people die in agonizing pain?

Response #7: I imagine that will be the case.

Question #8: After all this awful destruction, how is the "new world order" going to come about?

Response #8: (If they are honest with you, they will explain that the four-and-a-half million Jehovah's Witnesses must completely rebuild this earth, so that it becomes a paradise looking like the pictures contained in their publications.)

Question #9: It seems to me that the first thing the surviving Jehovah's Witnesses will have to do is to get rid of the five billion dead bodies lying all around! How is this going to be done, since dead bodies begin to decay and stink in just a day or so?

Response #9: Worms and birds are going to eat them up.

Question #10: You mean the first thing that the surviving Jehovah's Witnesses must do is stand around and watch the worms and birds eat those dead bodies?

Response #10: I guess so.

Question #11: This doesn't sound like it would be very enjoyable!

Response #11: We will endure for Jehovah's sake.

Question #12:   After the worms and birds have devoured all that flesh, you will still have to dispose of the skeletons, won't you?

Response #12:   Apparently so.

This is just part of one example of the many questions that you will find in Chapter Seven. After a Jehovah's Witness is probed like this, surviving Armageddon won't seem so wonderful to him. Without attacking their beliefs, you can help him to realize that what his instructors sold him on is really not that great.

• • • • • • • •

The ultimate goal of a Christian conversing with a Jehovah's Witness should be to lead him to personal faith in our wonderful Lord and Savior Jesus Christ. In Chapter Eight I have detailed the plan of salvation. This will make it easy for you to present all the steps in the plan of salvation: what sin is, the need for repentance, and proof that neither good works nor an organization can save, but that salvation comes only through being washed in the blood of the Lord Jesus Christ.

• • • • • • • • •

It is best not to make use of the Bible until you have gotten the ear of a Jehovah's Witness and he has begun to do some thinking for himself. Yet there are some Jehovah's Witnesses who will insist that you study the Bible with them. They might refuse to answer any questions about the organization. Of course, they only intend to use the parts of the Bible that they feel prove their teachings. So in Chapter Nine I show how you can use the Bible as an effective witness. You need to keep the J.W. on *un*familiar ground. I give suggestions on how you can control the direction of the conversation and decide what parts of the Bible to use. Again, I do not suggest you start with the Scriptures unless they refuse to let you question them about the organization.

• • • • • • • • •

There are several important steps in successfully witnessing to anyone in a cult. The first step is getting enslaved

Witnesses to realize that the Watchtower organization cannot be relied upon. This is possible by patiently asking unanswerable questions about their organization. To do this, you must first spend a lot of time in winning them to yourself. They need to realize that you are sincere and really interested in them as persons and that you have taken time to study their religion. Once they see they have been deceived, they will be hurt. Even so, it is usually difficult to get a cultist out of his religion and into another one right away. This is where the Christian needs to pray much. You need to keep on manifesting an interest in him as a person and show that you understand, to a degree, what he is going through. Chapter Ten is intended to give you ideas about ways to continue working with these wounded ones and, ultimately, lead them into a personal relationship with the Lord Jesus Christ. Remember, they have been taught many false ideas which need to be unlearned before they can begin to understand the truth.

The final step after bringing them to personal faith in the Lord Jesus Christ as their Savior is to get them to attend a Bible-believing church regularly. However, Witnesses have been brainwashed into expecting that the moment they enter a church building, Satan is sitting over the door and will jump on them—yes, that they will become demon possessed! Thus it can be excruciating for them to enter a church. They may be out of the Watchtower, but many of the Watchtower's myths and much of the awful fear that has held them fast is still not out of them.

•

For those who have close family members and friends in the Watchtower organization, Appendix I should prove helpful. It also will be useful to Christians who are meeting with Jehovah's Witnesses who insist on using their own material when they visit. You can turn the situation to your advantage, especially if you have a good grasp of the Watchtower's teachings. Appendix I explains how you can actually use Watchtower literature for witnessing effectively.

A Jehovah's Witness is always trying to get others to read Watchtower publications. By going along with his desire and reading their material, you have broken down one of the key barriers. But the Watchtower publications are written to be believed and accepted without questioning. They use a lot of double-talk. Their writings are anything but logical. Much of what they set forth in their publications cannot be explained. For people who are not emotionally involved and who think for themselves, it is readily apparent that what they present is not biblical. Reading their publications and asking questions on subjects for which your friends don't have the answers is a good way to cause them to think and question the Watchtower Society.

For this reason I have gone through the first part of the Watchtower book *You Can Live Forever in Paradise on Earth* and have pulled out many questions you may want to ask. (Witnesses like to use this book when starting their meetings in homes, as an introduction to the Watchtower's teachings.) I recall using these questions with a Jehovah's Witness elder, and even he did not have an answer for most of them. Using Watchtower literature this way can take a lot of pressure off your meetings with a Jehovah's Witness because they can't possibly get upset with you for asking reasonable questions about their own printed statements.

• •

The Watchtower Society has twisted and distorted the basic doctrines of Bible-believing Christians almost beyond recognition. For this reason, it is very hard for J.W.'s to understand truly biblical teachings. But once you help a Jehovah's Witness to realize that the Watchtower organization is not "the truth" and he begins to look for something else, it become essential to be able to expound some of the basic biblical doctrines. Appendix II therefore contains information on the Trinity, the personality of the Holy Spirit, the immortality of the soul, the 144,000, and the future home of the Christian. This section is not included to help you win an argument on these teachings when you first begin. Only after a Jehovah's Witness realizes that the Watchtower can't be relied upon and is sincerely seeking to know what biblical Christians believe, should this material be used.

• • •

Appendix III contains information about where you can buy additional source material on the Jehovah's Witnesses.

• • • •

It takes from six months to a year, or even longer, before a person becomes a Jehovah's Witness. It is, therefore, unrealistic to expect he will come out after only a few attempts at witnessing to him. It will take a lot of time, love, patience, study and prayer. I have many friends who used to be slaves of the Watchtower but are now "out." They declare that a Christian must have persistence if he is to be effective with a Jehovah's Witness. Remember, nothing can be compared to the joy of seeing someone come into new life through the Lord Jesus Christ. Culminating all your effort will be the fact that a person has been saved from the broad road that leads to eternal destruction and has entered the narrow road that leads to eternal life.

The ultimate aim of this book is to explain how the average Christian can be a successful witness for Christ. I cannot guarantee that you will always win the individual to Him, but you will have gained the opportunity to clearly present the plan of salvation after you have become a friend with him and won his confidence. Jehovah's Witnesses can be saved! God uses people like you to bring others to Christ! May the Lord strengthen you and encourage you as you read this book so that you might understand how to be a successful witness to those held in the strong grip of the Watchtower Society.

After reading this book, you may not want to wait until a Jehovah's Witness comes to your door. There are two ways you can initiate contact with them: (1) You can simply send a postcard to: Watchtower, 25 Columbia Heights, Brooklyn, NY 11201 and inform them that you are interested in their offer of having someone come to your home and discuss the

Watchtower organization. (2) Go to the local Kingdom Hall and invite someone to come. I have made several good contacts in this way. I would suggest that you go to the one-hour meeting which is held usually on Tuesday evenings; meetings on other evenings usually continue for two hours.

But perhaps you yet have a qualm: "I am a woman. I don't want a man visiting me." Fret not. In this matter Jehovah's Witnesses are very circumspect; they will not overstep the bounds of propriety. If you are a woman, the Kingdom Hall will be sure to send a woman (or perhaps two); if a man, one or two men. Or if you have made your contact as a couple, they will likely send a married couple to "enlighten" you.

As you turn the page and begin the next chapter, you will learn what to do on that all-important *initial encounter* with a Jehovah's Witness.

CHAPTER TWO

THE INITIAL CONTACT

It is ten o'clock on Saturday morning. It has been raining all week and the children are fit to be tied because they have had to stay in the house all week. But you promised them that you would go on a picnic today if the weather was good. How thrilled the children were when they woke up with the sun shining brightly into their rooms! Since breakfast, everyone has been busy. Some are making the sandwiches, others are getting out the folded chairs. As the preparations progress the excitement increases. Just when you are about ready, you go flying through the living room and happen to glance out the window. What you see causes you to stop in your tracks. A very nicely dressed man and woman with a seven-year-old boy, all carrying briefcases, are coming up the walk. "Oh, no! Here come those Jehovah's Witnesses. What are we going to do?"

This is a real dilemma for most Christians. It seems like the J.W.'s always come at an inappropriate time. Not only that, many Christians are not prepared to witness to them. This is understandable because there aren't any books out there to tell you what to do. So let us look at some typical approaches and see the effects.

Some people will run and hide and tell everyone to be quiet so the J.W.'s will think no one is at home. It may seem like a lifetime from the first knock to the time they leave. And when they do leave the front porch, they seem to walk very slowly down the drive and up to the next house. (The slower they walk, the fewer houses they have to visit.) After you think they are completely out of sight, you tell the children they can come out of hiding—and you feel you can now relax. You thought you got rid of them the easiest way possible. The only trouble is, there are ways of telling when people at are home and do not answer the doorbell. You undoubtedly forgot that your two cars were in the driveway and the trunk of one was open. Though you did not say one word to the Jehovah's Witnesses, they went away elated and encouraged because they knew you saw them and were hiding—and they interpreted this as proof that their arguments were obviously superior to yours. I know this is their reaction, because I have talked to a Jehovah's Witness elder about this very scenario.

Another typical approach is to answer the door and tell the Witnesses to go away because they are members of a false cult and of the devil. These Christians are likely to slam the door as hard as they can in the J.W.'s face. The flaw in this response is that the Watchtower has informed their followers that all Christians are rude. The Christian who has just slammed the door corroborates what the Witnesses have been told. I have been to their Kingdom Halls and heard them sing a song about going from door to door and how people will slam the door in their faces—but they will be "true to Jehovah because they are receiving persecution for His sake." (Yes, they do sing at a few of their five weekly meetings—not any of the traditional Christian hymns, of course, only songs of their making. They do not utilize a piano, but the music comes from a tape played over their speaker system. Nor do they sing these songs with any enthusiasm or gusto. This is merely another contribution to their dull meetings.)

Still other Christians will offer to listen to the J.W.'s for thirty minutes if the J.W.'s will listen to them for thirty minutes. When this is agreed upon, the J.W.'s will take their thirty minutes and then remember they have another appointment. They leave before the Christians get a chance to say anything. (The J.W.'s are too well indoctrinated to be changed in thirty minutes anyway.)

Another group of Christians will meet the J.W.'s at the

door, invite them in, and then run and get their Bibles. They begin to show them that Jesus is called God in John 1:1, and that it is a capital "G" in most Bibles. (In the Watchtower Bible it reads "a god.") Unknowingly they have run right into the J.W.'s trap. The J.W.'s love to attack the Trinity and are very well prepared. Christians beginning here are facing J.W.'s at their strongest point. Usually after thirty minutes to an hour of this, Christians give up because they don't seem to be making any headway. The Witnesses leave elated, feeling that their teaching is superior because they can stand up to the arguments of Christians. (John 1:1 is a very poor place to start since the J.W.'s are so well prepared; but at Isaiah 9:6 in their translation of the Bible, in this prophecy about Christ, it calls Him "Mighty God" and both "M" and "G" are in capitals.)

There is another very common reaction to the J.W.'s when they come to the door that seems very simple but plays into the Witnesses' hands. Many Christians will say, "I am a Christian and have my religion. I have no interest in yours, so good day," then politely close the door. The only problem with this is the Witness goes away greatly encouraged. Evidently the Christian knew the J.W.'s argument was superior to his and that was the reason the Christian didn't want to converse with him.

Is there any hope of getting through to Jehovah's Witnesses? Yes there is. But before I show you "a better way" I need to discuss a very common reason among Christians for not inviting a cultist into their house and witnessing to him.

Many Christians hesitate to invite a cultist into their homes because they feel it is forbidden by Scripture. Second John 10–11 says, "If there come any unto you, and bring not this doctrine [the doctrine of Christ, vv. 7–9], receive him not into your house, neither bid him God speed: for he that biddeth him God speed is partaker of his evil deeds."

For many years I turned cultists away from my door. However, I began to question my actions for three reasons:

1. Cultists are taught that Christians will be rude: our incivility is considered proof of the falseness of our religious profession. I only confirm this belief when I slam the door in their faces and refuse to talk to them.

2. I realized I was taking 2 John 10–11 out of context rather than harmonizing it with the rest of Scripture. Romans 12:20 instructs us: "Therefore if thine enemy hunger, feed him; if he thirst, give him drink; for in so doing thou shalt heap coals of fire on his head." And the Great Commission states in Matthew 28:19, "Go ye therefore, and teach *all* . . ." These verses seemed to contradict 2 John 10–11. So what was John really forbidding?

And what about John 3? Nicodemus, a Pharisee, came to Jesus and was welcomed by Him. The Pharisees and Jesus certainly were not in agreement. In fact, some of the strongest words that Jesus ever used were against the Pharisees' practices. Yet Jesus explained the way of salvation to Nicodemus, and he became a disciple of Christ.

3. I knew I was missing a great opportunity to witness. It isn't often that people come to one's door and want to converse about religion. And surely it is much easier to witness to someone while seated than to stand at the door and talk, especially when the weather is inclement.

One pastor who felt he should not invite cultists into his home has written about inviting them instead into his study at the church. But this created a problem for me. My study was in my *home*—not at church. I could not see the difference between inviting them into my home or into my study when both areas were under the same roof.

I began to do some serious thinking about this subject and found it helpful to learn about the culture and setting in which 2 John 10–11 was written. In Bible times, many inns were houses of ill repute. A traveling Christian would not want to stay in such a place of sin and temptation, so he needed to find lodging elsewhere. Paul often referred to the hospitality that he received, and he urged Christians to show hospitality to one another. Believers commonly opened their homes and provided a place for traveling Christians to stay. They placed the sign of a fish (much like we see on bumper stickers today) at the doorway of their houses to indicate that a Christian lived there. This sign made it easier for the Christian traveler to find lodging.

Also, many churches met in homes. There were traveling teachers who would come and speak at these house churches. The host would feed them and provide housing.

This was the setting in which 2 John 10–11 was written. Christians were to welcome fellow Christians, but they were not to provide free lodging for those who wanted to destroy the gospel. Christians were not to give false teachers an opportunity to present their teachings to the churches.

In short: these verses do not prohibit a Christian from inviting a person into his home for conversation. When you invite a cultist into your home you are not pronouncing a blessing upon him or giving him your approval, but using the opportunity to witness for Christ. (See note in the NIV Study Bible under 2 John 10.)

The same restrictions can be applied today. Do not offer free food or lodging to a cultist. Do not let him speak in your church. However, we can take advantage of their coming right to our doors to present the gospel to *them*.

Now I show you a better way.

When Jehovah's Witnesses are out going door to door, they are trying to make initial contacts that will lead into opportunities for further visits. This initial visit will usually be short, because the others in their group will be waiting for them. They will want to set up an appointment with you for a longer visit. This works to your advantage because you will need the longer time to present the plan of salvation to them.

Before you say anything to them about religion, you must first get a firm commitment from the individual(s) to come for at least *twenty visits*, more if possible. This is very important and one of the secrets in successful witnessing. If you do not get a definite commitment from them on this initial contact, they will not return once they have had their say and realize you know something about the Bible. Because they *like* to come back for a long period of time, however, they are usually very willing to make such a commitment.

They always have some sort of sales pitch, which might go something like this: "You know there is much evil in the world today, like war, crime, drugs, etc. Wouldn't you like to live in a perfect paradise here on earth?"

In order to get the commitment you want, you should very politely respond:

You: "I don't think I would be interested in discussing your concern today, because only one hour of my time discussing religion with you wouldn't begin to answer my questions." (Be sure to use the words "*one hour*.")

J.W.: "Oh, we could come back more than just one time."

You: "But I do have many questions."

J.W.: "We would love to answer your questions."

You: "I don't have any problems with the Bible itself but I do have many perplexing questions concerning your organization which probably would take a lot of time."

J.W.: "That is okay. We don't mind answering questions."

You: "I'm very busy. You have to realize I don't have much free time."

J.W.: "We could come for just one hour a week."

You: "For how long a period would you be able to come back?"

J.W.: "We can come back for as long as you want us to." (This is the kind of commitment that you want and need.)

You: "I'm not really sure. If I were to study with you, I would try to prepare so that I would not waste your time. If we met eight or ten times and things didn't go the way you anticipate, how do I know that you won't just break off the discussions and leave me stranded? This would be a waste of time for me."

J.W.: "Oh, we would never do anything like that."

You: "I'm not sure if I want to do this or not. I'll need some time to think about it and see if I can adjust my schedule. If you'll give me your name, address and phone number, I'll get in contact with you if I'm interested. If I do decide to meet with you, I would prefer to study with only one of you." (This begins to break down their support system.)

I am assuming here that you are speaking as an *individual*. But if you are responding as a husband and wife, then specify you would always want the same J.W. couple to visit. This request should not cause any problem.

However, if you are only an individual and the J.W. will not come unless there are two of them, then insist that the same two partners come back each time. You might say: "If different people were to come, it would make it much more difficult for us to make progress because a lot of time would be wasted in discussing material that has already been covered." (After coming for a while, if the J.W. brings a different partner it is imperative to tell them both at the door that you won't study with them that day. Tell the regular caller to be sure to bring along his or her original partner the next week. Even though they have agreed always to come together, they will very often try to get away with breaking their promise. One may say that the other is sick, or that it is inconvenient for him. But if you let them get away with changing partners, they often will keep changing and you won't be able to make much progress with the original persons.)

• • •

In the following chapter, I will show how you can begin your discussion by giving your personal testimony in a non-confrontational way—and what to do after that. But first, here are the seven marks of a cult.

1. CULTS REJECT ALL PARADOXES OF SCRIPTURE. Whenever a cultist encounters concepts in Scripture that seem to contradict each other, he accepts only one concept and rejects the other. Examples of such concepts are: Jesus as both God and man, divine election and human free will, the

mercy and wrath of God, and God's ability to be localized though omnipresent.

2. CULTS REJECT ANYTHING THEY CANNOT EX-PLAIN. For example, the Trinity, the deity of Christ, hell, and the immortality of the soul.

3. CULTS USE THE BIBLE—PLUS! Cults give other books equal authority with the Bible. These writings become the true basis for their beliefs. Jehovah's Witnesses use the Watchtower magazine and other Watchtower publications. They say that the only way the Bible can be understood is through their leaders' interpretation.

4. CULTS RECOGNIZE A MAN OR GROUP AS HAV-ING ABSOLUTE AUTHORITY. If a cultist fails to acknowl-edge the complete authority of his leaders, he is thrown out of the group. The leaders do not want anyone to question what they have to say.

5. CULTS DENY SALVATION BY FAITH ALONE. Cult-ists do not believe that a person can be saved by simple faith in Christ. They substitute a system of works which involves total subjection to the rules and regulations of the organization.

6. CULT LEADERS DO NOT WANT THEIR FOLLOW-ERS TO THINK FOR THEMSELVES. The leaders realize that if their followers read sound biblical literature or converse with outsiders who know the facts about their organization, the followers will begin to question what they have been taught. Therefore, the followers are forbidden to read such "apostate" literature or to talk to knowledgeable people.

7. CULTISTS MAKE IT DIFFICULT TO LEAVE THE OR-GANIZATION. Many members remain in a cult out of fear, having been told that the devil will take control of them if they stray. If a member will not submit to the organization or desires to leave, for whatever reason, he is disfellowshipped. Disfellowshipping cuts the person off from all contact with anyone still in the organization—even family members. Because a cultist rarely develops deep friendships outside the organiza-tion, disfellowshipping results in social and spiritual isolation. The Jehovah's Witnesses consider disfellowshipping to be

God's severest punishment. To a Jehovah's Witness, being disfellowshipped means that he will be annihilated at the time of death—will cease to have conscious existence—and will not be resurrected in the future with the rest of mankind.

Witnessing to a Jehovah's Witness is never easy, but we need to remember that he or she has an eternal soul and is lost without Christ.

CHAPTER THREE

HOW TO BEGIN

SET UP APPOINTMENTS

In order to deal successfully with a Jehovah's Witness over a period of time, you must follow some basic rules.

First, look at your calendar and decide on what day of the week you could best meet regularly with the Jehovah's Witness who has called at your door. Then phone him (or her) and set up an appointment.

When your visitor arrives, there are some things you need to settle and agree upon before you begin any discussion about religion. Be polite, but after the preliminary talk is over say, "When I spoke to you at the door I said that I had a number of perplexing questions about the Watchtower organization that might take some time. Your response was that you could come back for as long as I need. Is that correct?" You should receive an affirmative reply. Continue by saying, "I like people and do not want to have any hard feelings. I do not know how these discussions will go, but I want to make sure that we remain friendly with each other. So, if we could agree upon a few things, I am sure it would help in reaching this goal.

"1. I understand the purpose of these discussions is to talk about the Watchtower organization. As I said at the door, I do not have any problems with the Bible and I do not want to argue doctrine with you. Is that agreed? (Their whole approach is arguing doctrine and staying away from the Watchtower Society, so this is an important promise to get. Usually, at the outset your guest will agree to this proposal.)

"2. We will not attack other religious groups. This will

add nothing to our discussion. Just because another religion might be false, this does not make us right. (Witnesses spend most of their time attacking other religions. They think if they can prove all the other religious groups are "pagan"— then, by default, they are the true religion. By getting him to agree with this, you are taking one of his most effective weapons away from him. You will likely need to remind him of this promise several times along the way.)

"3. We want to keep to the issue of the Watchtower Society and not attack people. So I would like for us to agree that we will not stoop to character assassination. By this I mean accusing anyone of not being sincere, or saying you did not tell me all the facts at the beginning. (This is another important promise to get, because when a cultist is defeated and does not have an answer, he will almost always turn to character assassination. Thus you rob him of another of his tactics.)

"4. As I mentioned before, I prefer to study on a one-to-one basis with you. (If the Witness won't come unless there are two of them, then restate your insistence that the same two partners come all the time. Explain that if different people come, progress will be much slower because you will have to go over material that you have already covered. If two do come, a husband and wife combination is the best.)

"5. As you are aware, the Bible warns that there will be many false prophets and teachers in the last days. For this reason, I trust you won't mind if I do research as we study together. If we are lovers of the truth, there is nothing to fear from such an examination. (This sentence is a quote from one of their books. He should readily agree to this. Thus later on, if you want to use old Watchtower publications, he can't get upset with you because he has already agreed to your research.)"

After you have agreed on these basic rules, then you should set up appointments in advance. Take out a calendar and circle the dates that you agree upon for a couple of months. This is a visible reminder to him of his promise to come back over a period of time. If you don't get a firm commitment from him, he usually won't come back more than a few times. But it takes a lot longer than that to get him to see the error of the Watchtower Society and to explain to him the way of salvation through Christ. You might be able to give the gospel to him in words, but it will take time if he is to comprehend it.

A CLEAR VISION OF YOUR GOAL

To be successful in witnessing to a Jehovah's Witnesses you must understand why people join in the first place and what is the best approach in reaching them. I have never yet met a person who through reading the Bible arrived at conclusions that agreed with Watchtower teachings and then sought out an organization that had the same beliefs. With the exception of those raised in a Jehovah's Witness home, the reason most Witnesses joined was because of an emotional need. Perhaps they had just moved into the area and were lonely (the most common). Or they may have gone through a sickness, divorce, loss of job, death in the family, or a bitter experience with their church. They did not join the Watchtower Society because they really felt it was the best religion, but because someone was willing to show them some attention when they were in a time of need. They would easily have become a Mormon if the Mormons had gotten there first, or a true Christian if some Christian had shown them love and concern first.

At first Jehovah's Witnesses appear to be loving and concerned about others. But this is only true until they get the new person baptized and hooked in their religion. Every Jehovah's Witness has a great spiritual need and is empty. Even those who were born and raised a Witness have many problems with which they are struggling. They realize that the love and concern their religion once showed is no longer there. The Watchtower way has never met this emotional need, so you must speak to this need first. Offer them something more fulfilling and superior to what they have.

BECOME FRIENDS, TO MEET THE EMOTIONAL NEED

Begin the first appointment by learning as much as possible about the individual(s) who have come. This is important. The more you know about them, the better you will know how to approach them in your witnessing. Your concern and interest in learning more about them, their family, etc., will usually impress them. (Once a person is baptized as a Jehovah's Witness, the organization takes away all individual worth so the Witness now blends into the organizational worth.) If necessary, jot down notes from this part of the conversation. Review your notes before the next appointment so the person will sense that you cared enough to remember. I always *begin* my discussion with something personal and *end* on a personal note. It is important that you work hard to build a good relationship. This is one of my main thrusts during my first five appointments. (The other intent is to get them to think.) Once you have built a relationship, they will have confidence in you and will begin to open up and trust you. After this happens, hopefully they will be more willing to listen.

TAKE CHARGE OF THE CONVERSATION

Take charge of the conversation to prevent the Witness from hurrying into his preplanned presentation. (Remember it is your home, and you have a right to control the direction of the conversation. They often want to take over.) I do this by saying, "Before we get into the specifics on religion, I would like to discuss why each of us chose the religion that we did. Suppose you go first, and tell me why you became a Jehovah's Witness." By showing an interest in what attracted him to the Watchtower, it will give you a clue about his primary motivating factors and what he is really looking for in life.

Their explanation is usually brief. They often say, "I feel that the teachings of the Watchtower Society are more in line with what the Bible teaches and make more sense than the teachings of any other group." Others might say, "The world has many problems. We feel that the Watchtower Society has the answer to those problems."

If the individual did not grow up a Jehovah's Witness, ask him how long he studied with the Witnesses before he was baptized. Ask if he was reading the Bible on his own at the time he was studying—so that he could check all the references in their full context. (It is almost certain that the Witness did not read the Bible on his own, or he would never have become a Jehovah's Witness.) This will be valuable information later. The Bible says in 1 John 4:1–3 that we are to "test" a religion. Ask your visitor(s) in what way they studied the various pros and cons in obedience to Scripture. (It is obvious that they didn't, but let *them* see this.)

Though Jehovah's Witnesses seem so sold on the Watchtower way, many of them have questions about the organization—but it is impossible to discuss these with another Jehovah's Witness, who might squeal on them. This would result in their being taken before the elders for a severe scolding. They really have no friends, no one they can turn to. (I have a friend who used to be a Jehovah's Witness. When I first met him, he was one of their leading elders. Over a period of time he confided in me that during his twenty-eight years as a Jehovah's Witness he was never satisfied.)

If you show them real love and concern, they will respond to you. Thus you are apt to win a Jehovah's Witness to Christ more by your love and concern than through any profound arguments you can present about your faith.

SHARE HOW YOU BECAME A CHRISTIAN

After they have finished and you have asked the above-mentioned questions about their process of becoming a

Jehovah's Witness, it is your turn to tell how you came to know Jesus Christ as your personal Savior. Do not speak in general terms. Be specific. Instead of saying "I realized that I was a sinner," list specific sins such as pride, self-righteousness, selfishness, anger, jealousy, lying, and disobeying your parents.

Very briefly stated, my testimony goes like this.

I was born in Clearfield, in the central part of Pennsylvania. My parents were not Christians then, but my father always took us to Sunday School. Once I asked my mother a question about the Bible. She couldn't answer me, so I felt I couldn't get much help from my parents.

One night when I was six years old, as I lay in my bed, I thought, "What would happen if I died in my sleep?" I didn't know anything about the way of salvation at the time. I felt that I needed some special preparation to get into heaven, but I didn't know what. In order not to die in my sleep, I decided not to go to sleep. Of course, eventually I did fall asleep.

The same question came to me every night for a week. Though I was only six, it was very real to me. From that time on, I realized I was carrying a heavy burden. Every time I sinned, it became heavier. As my years in grade school progressed, the burden on my heart became even heavier. I wanted to get rid of this burden but didn't know how.

Some people said, "Just do the best you can, and since God is 'a God of love,' everything will be okay." This didn't satisfy me. If the way to get to heaven was to do more good things than bad, it seemed I naturally always did more bad deeds than good ones. It was a hopeless situation.

Once I entered junior high school, I not only was carrying this heavy burden of sin, but I could not see any reason for living. After all, why was man put on earth? I was not satisfied with my life and had few examples of people who were.

In the summer of 1942 we moved to Chester, Pennsylvania, where my father got a job working in the shipyard during World War II. A pastor of a small community church came visiting one August afternoon shortly after we moved in and invited our family to church. My father, four brothers, my sister, and I went the next Sunday. We almost doubled the attendance of the Sunday School. This was a gospel-preaching church where people diligently studied the Bible. I enjoyed going to Sunday School and soon became active in the young people's group.

The next year in October there was an evangelistic campaign in our city. The Saturday night before it began, our young people's group went downtown and gave out invitations to the meeting. I went to the meeting Tuesday night and about 3000 people showed up I felt good because maybe some people were there because I had given out invitations.

The evangelist began to speak on sin, but in a different way than I had ever heard it before. He did not talk about war, drunkards, thieves, etc., but said that pride, self-centeredness, selfishness, anger, wrath, lying, cheating, gossip, jealousy, covetousness, backbiting, disobedience to parents, fighting with brothers and sisters, etc., were awful sins before God. He didn't say we were just tainted with sin, but we were all ungodly, wicked sinners before God. This did not go down too well with me. I was considered a "good boy" in our area because my father was a strict disciplinarian. I knew I was not perfect, but to be called a wicked, ungodly sinner made me so angry I didn't hear anything else the evangelist said.

As I left the meeting that night, I determined that I would not go back to any more meetings that week. I wanted to forget everything that rude evangelist had said. But God had other plans.

As I went to bed that Tuesday night I recalled thirteen actual sins. I wasn't proud of this, but I also didn't think thirteen sins for a fourteen-year-old boy was too bad. Wednesday night as I went to bed, the Holy Spirit brought back more sins. My list grew from thirteen to twenty-five. Thursday night I began counting at twenty-six and got up to fifty. That night I thought, "Maybe that evangelist was right about my sins and I was wrong." Well, Friday night I settled the issue. I continued on from fifty-one and got up to one hundred. Then my whole past life exploded and the recollection of many more sins came pouring in upon me. These were not just general sin categories but actual sins. For the first time in my life I realized what a sinner I was before the holy and righteous God of the Bible. It was very humbling.

Fortunately, the next night I found the answer to my sin problem. Twice a month on Saturday night many young people from various churches in our city got together for a meeting. I went and was glad I did. The speaker's message was on sin, but this time I could not argue with him because God had revealed part of my sinful heart to me. "The Bible tells us," he said, "that Jesus Christ came into this world to save sinners. If we will acknowledge our sins and believe that Jesus Christ died on the cross for them, then we can be saved."

As I sat there, I said to myself, "Am I really hearing what this man is saying? He said I am an ungodly sinner. I know that's true. He also said Jesus Christ died for sinners. Since I am a sinner, then I qualify for the salvation that Jesus Christ is offering."

Right there I bowed my head, confessed my sins, and asked Jesus to come into my life and save me from my sins. At that very moment I felt the burden of my sins lifted. For the first time in my life I was free. Then I realized what was missing in my life. God created me to have fellowship with Himself, but sin had come in and separated me from God. I hadn't known the reason I had been created. That's why I lacked any purpose for living. When God took away my sins, He brought me into a living fellowship with Himself. I left the meeting that night with a light heart and a reason for living.

The next day, Sunday, as I went to church, it had a new and deep meaning for me. I will never forget when they talked about God being our Father—because now I knew Him in a personal way. Monday, as I entered school, I realized I was a different person and that God was going with me.

Having been taught that when you know Christ as your Savior you are to read your Bible and pray every day, this I began to do. What I read in the Bible surprised me because it was such a personal book. It was as if it were written just for me. I didn't realize then how God knew my heart so well. Of course the Word of God began to convict me of any sins I committed and had a cleansing effect on my daily life.

I usually take thirty minutes to give my testimony. I try to make it as interesting as possible. I want them to feel what I went through when I realized the heaviness of the burden of my sin. I want them to understand the relief I felt when I recognized and confessed my sins, trusted Jesus Christ as my personal Savior, and had this burden removed. I want them to long for the love, joy, and peace with God I experienced. They usually listen intently as I am giving my testimony, often siting on the edge of the couch.

One thing you will want to emphasize in your testimony is the personal relationship that you have with the Father through the Lord Jesus Christ. They have no relationship with the Father, nor the Son, so this is something very strange to them. You need to explain that when we recognize our sins, repent, and trust Christ as our own Savior we are born into the family of God and given eternal life. As children of God we never need to obtain this life again, but we will grow in the Lord as we read the Bible and obey Him. As children of God, there are times when we might be disobedient, but this does not cancel our "sonship" but only our fellowship. Confessing of our sins brings us back into fellowship.

The purpose of sharing your testimony is to very simply (but clearly) present the plan of salvation. By beginning the appointment this way, you can present the gospel to a Witness before he has had a chance to get his defenses up.

Getting acquainted and giving your testimony will take up your first session. On the next occasion, after talking about personal things you can begin by saying, "I'm glad I can talk with you. I don't have much trouble understanding the Bible, but I do have trouble understanding the Watchtower organization. I have many questions about the organization and its teachings that I hope you can answer for me." The following chapters in this book explain how to continue.

No matter how well the conversation seems to be going, never, never, never talk more than forty-five minutes to an hour on religious matters. If you talk more than that, you will give him too much and it could easily drive him away. Give your visitor plenty of time to think about what you have discussed. You can spend as much time as you like before or after your discussion in making friends. This is something I would encourage.

"DO NOT'S" IN WITNESSING TO JEHOVAH'S WITNESSES

DO NOT BE IMPOLITE. Getting into an argument with them will not do any good and may even hurt your cause.

DO NOT START OUT BY ATTACKING THEM AND THEIR RELIGION. It is only natural for a Jehovah's Witness to start defending when he feels he is being attacked. The approach of this book is to ask them thought-provoking questions to get them thinking. If through your questions you can cause them to think and get them involved in coming to the conclusion that their organization is not reliable, then there is a better chance of them leaving the Watchtower Society.

Let me give you an illustration. Suppose my son is looking for a car. He has been looking for a long time and finds something he thinks he likes. He asks me to go along and see what I think, because I have had some experience at buying cars (twenty to be exact). I spot the defects in the vehicle easily. If I say, "You are really stupid to pick out a piece of junk like this! Don't you have any brains at all?" he probably will be defensive and be all the more determined to buy the car, just to prove me wrong.

There is another way. I can look the car over. I can then point out that the tires are not good and ask him to examine them. As I scan down the side of the car, I may notice that it has been in an accident. I can explain to my son how one can spot this.

We take the car for a ride. The transmission doesn't sound too good. I ask my son what that sound is, and he comes to the conclusion that it is the transmission. After we get back to the used car lot, we check the date of the last oil change. This was recent. We notice that the oil is down, which means it burns oil.

About this time my son probably will say, "Dad, I don't think this would be too good of a buy. What do you think?" He has reached the conclusion I wanted him to reach, but it was his decision.

This is the same thing I want to do with Jehovah's Witnesses. If I call their religion stupid, it will only make them more determined—because the organization has taught them that all opposition is from the devil. If I patiently ask them questions, however, they will come to the conclusion that it is not God's true organization and will be apt to leave.

DO NOT LET THEM GET YOU INTO THE POSITION WHERE YOU ARE JUST DEFENDING YOUR BELIEFS. The proselyting method of the Jehovah's Witnesses is not just to relate what they believe, but to try to get you confused when you are defending your Christian beliefs. They are usually not in a house more than five minutes before they will say that the teaching of the Trinity, the immortality of the soul, the doctrine of hell, the idea that all people may go to heaven, and such, are pagan beliefs and of the devil. They want to get on the Trinity doctrine right away, and are usually successful by this approach.

They are not trying to get you to defend your teachings so that they may really know what you believe. They think they *already* know. Therefore, do not feel elated when they begin to ask you about your beliefs and presume you will be the first person to get through to them. They concur with the Watchtower in avowing that all other religions are members of "Babylon" and of the devil. The Watchtower publications have perverted the beliefs and actions of Christians. Though Jehovah's Witnesses will ask you about your beliefs, they will never patiently listen while you explain. They will keep interrupting and asserting that your faith is built on false ideas. They are trying to get you confused and to divert you from asking questions about their religion. You may feel like responding that no one has the right to come into your house and challenge your beliefs. (In most cases J.W.'s *are* successful in getting Christians to defend their beliefs; but no one can win a war by just *defending*.)

It is much better to ignore their attacks and question them on their organization. In this way you are the one in control of the conversation. Then they will hear what you say and be more ready to accept it. At the beginning they are only hearing sounds when you speak; they are not really listening. And when you stop talking and the sound ceases, they know that they can begin talking again.

DO NOT REACH FOR YOUR BIBLE IMMEDIATELY OR LET THEM START USING THEIRS. The Witnesses who go door to door are very well trained. By repeated drilling in their meetings, they have been taught most of the verses that Christians use. They have also been shown how to refute these verses. They don't have to do any personal thinking— they know their speech from memory. If you start using Bible verses at the very beginning, they will really not be listening to you to understand and accept the meaning of the verses as you understand them. They will simply be thinking of a verse to refute yours. And this will continue until you become very frustrated. It will be like Bible Ping-Pong.

You see, for the Christian, the Bible is the final authority, but for the Jehovah's Witness their "governing body" is the final authority. It doesn't really matter what the Bible clearly says because they only believe what the organization tells them a verse means. And the organization twists the meaning of verses to make the verses mean what the organization wants them to mean. A verse to which the organization hasn't given any meaning must be taken back to the organization to seek the meaning they give the verse. A Christian is considered pagan by a Jehovah's Witness, so anything he says will be thought of as the devil's interpretation.

They do not, nor can they, at first, think for themselves. When they become a Jehovah's Witness their mind is locked up and from then on is manipulated completely by the puppet strings of the Watchtower. They no longer think for themselves. They only believe what the organization tells them. If a person does not think for himself for a long period of time, it is impossible for him to think quickly. For this reason, you must spend some time getting them to think before you can use the Bible effectively. I firmly believe that the Bible is the Word of God and is powerful, but you must get a person ready to accept the Bible as the absolute authority before your use of the Bible will be effective. (All farmers know that a field must be plowed before seed can be sown.) Begin with the questions outlined in this book. I designed the questions to get them to *think* and to evoke a favorable response from them.

DO NOT USE GREEK AND HEBREW EVEN IF YOU KNOW EXACTLY WHAT YOU ARE TALKING ABOUT. Most Jehovah's Witnesses do not know Greek or Hebrew, but they think they know more than the average person so they will try to use it. Because it will only confuse the conversation, ask them not to use Greek or Hebrew. The Watchtower Society did not come into its beliefs by studying the original texts. They had their beliefs first and then tried to twist the Greek and Hebrew to mean what they wanted it to say. (Many illustrations to prove this point could be given.) It is interesting that the Jehovah's Witnesses do not have any real Greek or Hebrew scholars. They will quote many other scholars, mostly out of context, but never do you hear of a Jehovah's Witness who is a Greek or Hebrew scholar—because there are none. If there were any and they were honest men, they could not be Jehovah's Witnesses.

DO NOT START WITH JOHN 1:1 AND THE TRINITY. The Watchtower Society has put forth their greatest effort in trying to refute the Trinity, and Jehovah's Witnesses are very well prepared to discuss this. They have a thirty-two page booklet titled *Should You Believe in the Trinity?* They have explained away every verse that a Christian will use in trying to prove the Trinity, plus a few of which you might not be aware. They have given an answer to all your reasons for believing the Trinity. It is true they have twisted the meaning of the verses, but they have prepared their members to discuss the subject better than the true Christian is prepared to. They have over one hundred quotes in this booklet and feel they prove conclusively that the Trinity is a pagan doctrine. Yet every quotation, except one, is taken out of context, and they regularly quote only a small portion of the particular article, frequently giving just the opposite meaning from what the author intends. A good portion of the partial quotes are from articles written to *prove* the Trinity. A Christian might get a few points in, but you won't make much progress with them. As I said before, they are not really listening to you. They have gone over it so often that they can discuss the issue without even thinking.

Most Jehovah's Witnesses have never read a true article on the Trinity and only believe what the Watchtower Society tells them. The Watchtower says the Trinity is a pagan teaching—making God out to be a three-headed monster. They say that Trinitarians teach there are three gods in one, one god in three, and Jesus is the Father. This is so far from the truth that it is even hard to conceive how they ever came up with such an idea.

Most Christians believe that the Trinity is an important subject because it is the very foundation of Christianity. They believe they ought to begin here. There is no doubt the Trinity is important, but a person does not have to understand the Trinity to be saved. I don't know if I ever heard the word "Trinity" before I was saved. If they ask you whether you believe in the Trinity, it is best to say, "I believe in the one true God who is manifested by the name Yahweh." If they ask you to explain more, just stick to this answer. There is no way that a Jehovah's Witness can argue with this answer.

Sometimes they just will not take no for an answer. They will persist in trying to get you to discuss the Trinity. Here be firm and say, "I really don't have any problem with the Trinity, so there is no reason for me to discuss it with you. I am not a theologian and this is a theological question. [Even if you are, avoid arguing with them.] We agreed before that we would not argue doctrine. If *you* have a problem with the Trinity, then I would suggest that *you* go to a library and study up on the subject. The library has many good books on the subject and they can help you solve your problems."

The Jehovah's Witness' basic problem is not with the Trinity, but with sin. When we deal with most unsaved people, we start with sin. Jesus can only save sinners. I cannot understand where the idea came from that we must treat Jehovah's Witnesses differently than other sinners and begin with the Trinity. Once we get a Jehovah's Witness to realize that he is an ungodly sinner before God and he accepts Jesus as his personal Savior, the Holy Spirit will lead him into the truth about the Trinity as he reads the Bible. But before you can effectively approach Jehovah's Witnesses on the subject of sin, you must show them that their present savior, the Watchtower Organization, is not trustworthy. Only then will they look at the true Savior.

DO NOT START WITH THE SUBJECT OF HELL AND

THE 144,000. Jehovah's Witnesses are taught that to believe in the doctrine of hell you must believe that God created people so that He could just dangle them over the fires of hell and then gloat because they are suffering. You will have a hard time trying to convince them, at first, that this is not what you believe nor what the Bible teaches.

DO NOT PUT TOO MUCH PRESSURE ON THEM TOO FAST. There is always a tendency to try to get a decision from them too quickly. As I said before, it takes them a while before they really begin to hear you and begin to think. After that they still have to wrestle with what you are saying and to accept it as the truth. Even if we know we are wrong about something, it usually takes time for us to admit it. It is especially so with one who has been drawn into a false religion. Also, do not keep insisting on your point too long at a time. This often leads to an argument. It is best to back off for a little while and go to something else. Remember, you just want to get them to think. You don't have to win the argument.

DO NOT TELL THEM WHAT LOCAL CHURCH YOU BELONG TO. When they ask you what church you attend, I suggest you reply, "I only know of one church. That is the universal church of Christ." This usually will not satisfy them because they like to argue about different denominations. If they keep pushing the subject you can reply, "When you first came to my door, you mentioned about all the crime and wickedness in the world today. For this reason, I do not tell strangers personal things."

There is another reason I suggest you not give the name of your local church. It is my dream and desire that many Christians in a church will become active in witnessing to Jehovah's Witnesses. When this happens, if word were to get out to Jehovah's Witnesses that Christians from the "First Church" know what they are talking about, a Jehovah's Witness would never continue a conversation with you the moment he found out you were from the First Church. I want Christians to get in contact with the Jehovah's Witnesses so that they can witness to them rather than drive them away.

DO NOT USE OLD WATCHTOWER MATERIAL TOO QUICKLY, UNANNOUNCED, OR TOO MUCH AT A TIME. Some readers of this book may have old Watchtower material that shows the changes and contradictions in the Watchtower beliefs and actions. This material can be used ever so effectively in witnessing, but it must be used in the proper way. (If you do not possess any of this material, I have many copies of old Watchtower literature and I explain in Appendix III how you can order it.) If you use too much too fast, you will scare them away because they will realize you know too much. I heard of one case where a Christian had hundreds of pages which he used in his first encounter with a Jehovah's Witness. It didn't work out too well! It is best to wait until you have made friends with them and they have begun to do a little thinking for themselves. This takes at least six to ten visits, and even then I recommend you do not bring Watchtower literature out before you talk about it a little ahead of time.

In my discussion with a Jehovah's Witness, when a subject comes up on which I have some old material that I could use effectively I say, "It seems that I read something different on this subject. I want to be sure of what I am talking about. I will look it up and have it next week." Then the next week you have a good reason for presenting the old material you have on that subject.

For instance, they now teach that Christ began to reign invisibly in the heavens in 1914. However, for fifty years they taught that it was in 1874. So when I am talking with a Jehovah's Witness and the 1914 date comes up, I mention that I think I read somewhere that they used to teach Christ began to reign in 1874. This gives me a legitimate reason for doing research. Then, while I am researching this, I usually find more facts that I can use later. It is often best to use material you can find at a local library, the first time. For example, the name "Jehovah" is a false rendering for the name of God and is more properly rendered "Yahweh." This information can be found in any dictionary or encyclopedia.

After you have presented old Watchtower material several weeks in a row, it is often best to give them time to think about this material before you use any more.

DO NOT ARGUE AND GET INTO A HEATED DEBATE. Jehovah's Witnesses at first will be very polite, but when things do not go their way they can become very cantankerous and argumentative. They seem to thrive better when they can get you to argue. When you realize this is happening, you can say, "Stop." Don't say anything for a couple of seconds. Give yourselves a little time to calm down. Then you can remind them of the ground rules: that you do not want to argue and that we should be more careful to keep the conversation calm.

When a Jehovah's Witness realizes that he is not making progress, he will often become mean and nasty on purpose. The reason for this is to get you upset so that you will say, "I don't have to take this. Get out of here and don't come back anymore!" In this way the Christian has broken off the conversation and not him. If this happens, you should try to be all the more polite and not let him succeed in his tactics.

DO NOT TELL THEM OUTRIGHT WHAT YOU THINK OF THE WATCHTOWER SOCIETY. This will only hinder your cause. You want them to come to the same conclusion that you have about the Watchtower Society, but you want them to come to this conclusion as a result of your thought-provoking questions and not because you have told them outright.

I had been dealing with one Jehovah's Witness a long time. One night he said, "If what you have been showing me is true, then the Watchtower is wrong." (I had been able to show him some old Watchtower literature.) I had never said to him that the Watchtower was a false religion. He came to this conclusion himself.

DO NOT BE DISCOURAGED. There is a tendency to start out all enthused, but when you realize that it is going to take a lot longer than you thought, there is the temptation to quit. You need to realize that most Jehovah's Witnesses are poker-faced. It is hard to tell from their outward expressions what is really happening inside them. Even though they do not respond as quickly as you think they ought, it is important for your testimony that you continue meeting with them. If they realize that you are interested in them as a person and are not just seeking to gain some brownie points or put another notch on your conversion stick, they are more likely to respond.

WHAT TO DO IF YOU ONLY HAVE A FEW MINUTES OR DON'T WANT TO GET INVOLVED

The thrust of this book is to encourage Christians to deal with Jehovah's Witnesses over a period of time so that we will have the opportunity to lead them to a personal faith in the Lord Jesus Christ. Still, if you feel you do not want to get involved, there are *two* ways that take only a few minutes and will enable you to make a positive witness without arguing.

APPROACH #1: After they have given their sales pitch—usually something about a future paradise here upon this earth—you can very politely and courteously say, "You are a Jehovah's Witness aren't you!" Continue by saying, "You people study the Bible, don't you?" Then say, "I have a question about just one verse in the Bible. In the light of present-day Watchtower teachings, would you explain John 5:24 to me?" (Let them open their Bible and read it, because it says the same thing in their Bible.) It reads: "Most truly I say to you, He that hears my word and believes him that sent me has everlasting life, and he does not come into judgment but has passed over from death to life."

There is no way that this verse can be harmonized with Watchtower teaching. Ask them what this "everlasting life" is and how one can be sure of having it right now as this verse says. It obviously is something that a person can have in this present life. (According to the Watchtower Society, no one can have eternal life until after the thousand-year reign of Christ. No one can be certain of receiving it even then, because it is something they feel they will merit because of a faithful life and there is always the possibility that they might fall away before that time comes.) Through this question, you are saying in silent words that the Bible teaches we can have eternal life right now.

Ask them what it means to "not come into judgment." (Jehovah's Witnesses do not believe in a soul, so to them "judgment" is physical death. To them it has to mean that they will not die. We know many Jehovah's Witnesses have died, so this is obviously not the answer.) Ask them to explain what this death *is* that the person has passed out of, and what *is* this life they have entered. (Since the Watchtower religion does not believe that man has a soul, there is no spiritual death. To them it could only mean resurrection from *physical* death, and obviously this is not the right answer.)

I am almost 100% sure they cannot explain this verse. They will usually say that they can't answer it but will come back later with an answer. (But more than likely they won't come back.) Though this type of question takes only a few minutes, without preaching you can send them away thinking about a powerful verse and a few important thoughts.

I remember talking to a man who had been a Jehovah's Witness for over forty years before he was saved. I asked him if he remembered any thought-provoking incidents when he was going from door to door during this time. Without hesitating he went back about thirty-three years and mentioned an almost similar brief conversation that he had with a Christian woman. It left an unforgettable impression upon him. She asked him, "Why does Jesus feel it so important that a man must be born again?" He couldn't answer her, but he kept thinking about it.

APPROACH #2:   After their sales pitch, begin your conversation this way: What you have said about world conditions is true. Since you have an interest in a better future, may I ask you a couple of questions?

Response: Of course.

Question #1: Do you spend a lot of time studying the Bible?

Response: Yes.

Question #2: Do you believe that we are all ungodly sinners before God?

Response: Yes, we believe that no one is perfect and we all have our faults.

Question #3: Do you believe that pride, self-centeredness, selfishness, anger, wrath, lying, cheating, gossip, jealousy, covetousness, backbiting, drinking, adultery, lust, fighting with brothers and sisters, disobedience to parents, etc., are sins before Almighty God?

Response: Of course they are.

Question #4: Do you believe that Jesus Christ shed His blood and died for sinners?

Response: Yes.

Question #5: Do you believe that there is another life after this one?

Response: Yes.

Question #6: I came to the place in my life where I realized that I was an ungodly sinner before God and a child of the devil. When I realized this, I no longer wanted to continue on this road. I believe that the Bible is the Word of God and teaches that the Lord Jesus Christ shed His blood and died for sinners. I knew that I was a sinner. Since Jesus Christ died for sinners, then I qualified for the salvation that He provided. I confessed my sins to God, repented, and asked the Lord Jesus Christ to come into my heart and save me from my personal sins. He was true to His word and took away my heavy burden of sin and forgave my sins. When I believed that Jesus is the Christ and acted upon this truth, I was born into the family of God. God gave me the gift of eternal life.

Once this eternal transaction took place in my heart, I began to read the Bible to find out what a born-again child of God should do, because I wanted to live according to the

Father's will. The Bible was not difficult after I was saved because the Spirit of God led me into its truths. It is now my desire to have nothing to do with the world and live only for the glory of Yahweh.

When I trusted Christ as my personal Savior, I became a member of God's organization. I believe in only one true and living God who is known by His personal name, Yahweh. Since I have come to know the good news of salvation through the Lord Jesus Christ, my great desire is that this good news of the kingdom should be proclaimed from door to door throughout the whole world. Because of the forgiveness of sins I received through the Lord Jesus Christ, the Holy Spirit wrote my name in the "Lamb's book of life." For this reason, I know that I will go to dwell with Yahweh for all eternity. I also believe that King Jesus will rule over this earth for a thousand years.

Could you please tell me what is wrong with a faith like this? (Note: Jehovah's Witnesses think they are the only ones who are doing God's will, belong to God's organization, use God's personal name, preach the good news of the kingdom from door to door throughout the world, and believe that Jesus will reign over this earth for one thousand years. Thus they will be greatly surprised at what you have said.)

Response: That is fine. Good day. (Actually, it is impossible to know just what the response will be, but in these few minutes you have been able to present the whole plan of salvation in terms that a Jehovah's Witness should understand. Since you gave your testimony in the form of a question, they were listening. You were able to give them many things to make them think.)

Before I explain more fully what Jehovah's Witnesses believe, I am going to give a brief history of the Watchtower organization.

CHAPTER FOUR

HISTORY OF THE WATCHTOWER MOVEMENT

Charles Taze Russell, founder of the Watchtower Society, was born in Allegheny, Pennsylvania, in 1852. He was raised in the Presbyterian Church. He later joined the Congregationalist Church, but left because he was against the doctrine of eternal punishment. After hearing an Adventist speak, Russell was taken up with their teaching that hell was the "common grave." He then began to teach and preach that there was no consciousness after death until the resurrection. He began a small Bible study in 1872, but 1879 is the date given as the beginning of his movement.

Russell was interested in the work of N. H. Barbour of Rochester, New York. Barbour taught that Christ would return in 1874—in spite of the fact that Matthew 24:36 says, "But of that day and hour knoweth no man, no, not the angels of heaven, but my Father only." When Christ did not return in 1874, Barbour said that the return was "invisible." This was Barbour's way of covering up a false prophecy.

Barbour had studied the works of John Aquila Brown (an Englishman) and adopted much of Brown's interpretation. However, Barbour soon changed the date for Christ's return to 1914—when Christ was to come to earth to set up His millennial kingdom. Barbour claimed that the 1874 invisible return was a preliminary one that was necessary before His visible return in 1914. He published the 1914 date in July, 1877, in the book *Three Worlds,* page 83. It has been a central teaching of the Watchtower Society since then.

In 1878, Russell and Barbour began publishing a magazine, *The Herald of the Morning,* which later became *The Watchtower* magazine. Russell broke with Barbour in 1884 and formed Zion's Watch Tower Tract Society. He later changed the name to Watchtower Bible and Tract Society, which is still in use today. The members of the Society are commonly known as Jehovah's Witnesses and their meeting places as Kingdom Halls.

Russell, using Barbour's date, said that the Battle of Armageddon would take place in 1914 (*Studies*, Vol. II, pp. 98–99, 101, and Vol. III, pp. 126 and 153). This battle would result in the destruction of the world powers and the beginning of the millennium. When Christ did not return as predicted, Russell said that Christ began to reign in the "heavens" and that shortly the world would end. We know, however, (from Philippians 2:9–11 and other passages) that Christ has been reigning since He returned to heaven following His resurrection from the dead.

Russell denied the Trinity, the deity of Christ, the bodily resurrection of Christ, the deity and personality of the Holy Spirit, the existence of hell, and the consciousness of man after death. He taught that all religions, including Christendom, were in darkness. He said that only the followers of his teachings were right in their beliefs.

Charles Russell died on October 31, 1916. The present-day Jehovah's Witnesses deny many of his teachings. They do not completely reject him, but they will not sell his books. They say that he made many mistakes in his interpretation of Scripture. When the Jehovah's Witnesses quote Russell, they distort his teachings to support their current beliefs.

J.F. Rutherford (commonly known as Judge Rutherford, though he was never a judge) succeeded Russell as the spiritual head of the organization. Rutherford was born in Missouri in 1869 and joined the movement in 1906. Many Russellites did not like Rutherford and left. Those who stayed tried to develop an organization that worked like a machine, cranking out literature to spread the Watchtower teachings.

Continuing the date-setting of Russell, Rutherford said that the world would end in 1925. In his book *Millions Now Living Will Never Die*, he said:

As we have previously stated, the great jubilee cycle is due to begin in 1925. At this time the earthly phase of the kingdom shall be recognized. . . . Therefore we may confidently expect that 1925 will mark the return of Abraham, Isaac, Jacob, and the faithful prophets of old, particularly those named by the Apostle in Hebrews chapter eleven, to the condition of human perfection. (1920, pp. 89–90)

The fact that Rutherford's prediction did not come true shows him to be a false prophet.

In 1930, the Watchtower Society built a mansion, Beth-Sarim (House of the Princes), in San Diego, California. They expected the Old Testament prophets to return to live there. Rutherford lived in the mansion for many years.

In 1931, at a convention in Ohio, Rutherford gave his followers the name "Jehovah's Witnesses." They base the name on Isaiah 43:10a, which says, "Ye are my witnesses, saith the LORD, and my servant whom I have chosen." They ignore the second half of the verse which says, "that ye may know and believe me, and understand that I am he: before me there was no God formed, neither shall there be after me"—for they teach that Jesus was formed by the Father, and that in the future He will become a "Mighty God."

Rutherford died at Beth-Sarim on January 8, 1942. After his death, they elected Nathan H. Knorr as the third president of the Watchtower Society. Knorr was born in Bethlehem, Pennsylvania, in 1905. He became a member at the age of eighteen.

During his administration the Watchtower published their own translation of the Bible, called the New World Translation. They released it in sections between 1950 and 1961. Prior to this translation, they had been using the King James Version or the American Standard Version of the Bible. They now call those versions "the devil's Bible." The New World Translation was written in such a way that it supports their beliefs in crucial texts that previously had caused them problems.

Also under Knorr, the Society strengthened its proselytizing efforts and developed successful training programs for producing new workers for the Watchtower movement. Knorr died in June, 1977, at the age of seventy-two.

For many years one man ran the organization: first Russell (1879–1916), next Rutherford (1917–1942), and then Knorr (1942–1977). However, during Knorr's term of leadership, in the early 1970's, a number of influential men forced the president and vice-president to accept a governing body made up of about thirteen men. To be a member of the governing body a person must have been a baptized Jehovah's Witness before 1935. Those who joined before 1935 are known as the "anointed class" which is to make up the 144,000. Since there are not many of these Jehovah's Witnesses left, the policy must be changed in the near future. They will call the change "receiving new light."

Frederick W. Franz became the fourth president of the Watchtower in 1977. Though he did not have the same power as the previous presidents, because of the governing body forced upon the organization in the early 1970's, his influence was still very strong. He was born in Covington, Kentucky, on September 12, 1893. He came in touch with the Jehovah's Witnesses through an older brother. He then was attending the University of Cincinnati, preparing to become a Presbyterian minister. Instead, he separated from the Presbyterian Church and became associated with the Bible Students, as Jehovah's Witnesses were then called. He was baptized on November 30, 1913, and the following year he left the university and entered the colporteur work. He went to the Brooklyn headquarters in 1920 and remained there the rest of his life until his death on December 22, 1992, at the age of 99. Franz was primarily responsible for making verses in the New World Translation of the Bible conform to Watchtower teachings.

As early as 1966, Franz predicted that Christ would return in 1975 (*Life Everlasting—in Freedom of the Sons of God*, 1966, pp. 29–30). In anticipation of this event many people sold their homes, and some sold their businesses so that they could use the money to work full time spreading the Watchtower message.

When the prophecy proved to be false, the Society said that people had misunderstood what they had written. It wasn't until four years later that the Watchtower Society admitted their error. Following this, many people left the organization.

For a while, growth of the Watchtower Society slowed, especially in the United States. However, expansion continued in other countries. The Society causes a great deal of confusion in these countries because many people—not realizing that the Jehovah's Witnesses are a false cult—classify them under true Christianity. They use high-pressure tactics to get people to study Watchtower publications.

They named Milton G. Henschel the fifth Watchtower president on December 30, 1992, at the age of 72. He was born a third-generation Jehovah's Witness in Pomona, New Jersey, and was baptized in 1934. He has served for some fifty years at the Brooklyn headquarters and was vice-president under Franz for several years. As a younger man he was personal secretary to the Society's third president Nathan Knorr, but later had a falling-out with him. Eventually, as a member of the governing body during the final years of Knorr's presidency, he cared for administrative work. He is a conservative and against change. However, it is almost certain that he must introduce some major doctrinal changes because the 1914 and 1935 dates have both just about run out.

The teachings and practices of the Jehovah's Witnesses have changed greatly under the five respective leaders. Most Watchtower publications over ten years old are outdated and are no longer used. The beliefs that "prove" they are the only true religion are different from their beliefs of fifty years ago. However, *truth will not and cannot change.*

You will need to know and remember something about the two dates 1914 and 1919, because these are central in their teachings.

They now teach that 1914 was the turning point in history and the date when Christ began to reign invisibly in the heavens. This marked the beginning of the end time. They speak about the increase of famines, earthquakes, wars, etc., since 1914 as proof that this was a significant date. (Yet when one checks the facts, there is no proof at all that there has been an increase in these signs since 1914.) All Jehovah's Witnesses must accept this 1914 date or they will be disfellowshipped.

The date 1919 is important because they claim that at this time God looked over all the religious organizations then existing and found that the Watchtower Society was the purest organization. At this time He appointed them to be His "faithful and discreet slave" (See Matt. 24:45–47). They claim that they are "God's sole channel of communication to this earth." The reason they chose this date was because on June 21, 1918, Joseph Rutherford and six other leaders were imprisoned on "sedition charges" because of some of the things they wrote about World War I. The officials released them on March 25, 1919, which they claim showed that God's favor was upon their organization again.

The changes in their teachings through the years show that the Society is not "the channel of God's communication" to the world as they claim. In spite of the changes, they expect members to be in complete agreement with the Society's teachings and to be in complete obedience to the organization.

CHAPTER FIVE

THE CONTRAST BETWEEN BIBLICAL CHRISTIANITY AND WATCHTOWER BELIEFS

Second Peter 3:16b says, "His [Paul's] letters contain some things that are hard to understand, which ignorant and unstable people distort, as they do the other Scriptures, to their own destruction" (NIV).

Jehovah's Witnesses (like any other cultists) are masters at distorting Scripture to fit their beliefs. If a person tries hard enough, he can make the Bible say almost anything. To confuse people, Jehovah's Witnesses use the words and terms of Christianity but change the meanings to suit themselves. Much of what they say sounds good until you learn how they define the terms they are using.

A Jehovah's Witness usually will not give you a clear definition of their terms because he knows that if you find out the truth about what they believe you will not give him an opportunity to present the Society's teachings. Even their publications cannot be taken at face value. It took a lot of research for me to discover what the Jehovah's Witnesses really believe. This chapter will present those beliefs.

So that you can properly compare biblical Christianity with the unbiblical beliefs of the Watchtower Society, I will first present the orthodox beliefs and then the teachings of the Watchtower Society. (A more detailed explanation of some of the doctrines will be given in Chapter Six.)

ORGANIZATION

Biblical Christianity. Salvation comes directly from

God as a gift when one accepts Jesus Christ as his personal Savior. This makes him a born-again child of God and places him into the true universal body of Christ. Joining a church or organization will not save anyone, but all true believers should become active members of a Bible believing and preaching church. While there are many denominations and fellowships, the Bible nowhere teaches that there is only one central organization upon this earth, run by a man or group of men, through which God channels His message, illumines Scripture, and sets down binding rules and regulations which must be followed to obtain salvation.

Jehovah's Witnesses. They teach that Jehovah God has always had one central organization upon this earth through which He channels all communication to man. *They claim to be that organization.* All persons must be active members of the Watchtower Society to gain God's favor and must work for their salvation. This work mainly consists of being one hundred percent in submission to all the rules and regulations (right or wrong) of the Watchtower Society.

Understanding their idea of "organization" is essential to understanding the Jehovah's Witnesses because everything they believe and practice is determined by its governing body and not by the Bible, though they use Bible verses taken out of context to try to prove their own preconceived ideas. They teach that we need both a "father" and a "mother." They say that Jehovah God is the Father and the Watchtower organization is the visible "mother." To a Jehovah's Witness, when the organization speaks it is just like God speaking. If one refuse to believe and obey everything that the organization teaches, it is like blaspheming God Himself. They teach that all other religious organizations, denominations, and churches are apostate, and part of "Babylon the Great" which is ruled by Satan and under the condemnation of God.

They teach that the apostles of Christ made up a governing body with the same kind of power with which the

Watchtower Society rules. They use Acts 15, where it speaks about the council at Jerusalem, to try to prove there was a governing body that had the power to form policies and dictate them to all Christians. However, when one looks closely at Acts 15, it is not a pattern for a human organization. There were certain men from Jerusalem teaching that the Gentiles must be circumcised and keep the laws of Moses to be saved (vv. 1 and 5). From verse 7, which says "And when there had been much disputing," it is evident that some at this council held very strongly to this erroneous idea. Paul, Barnabas, and others who were not apostles went up to Jerusalem and called the apostles and elders together to correct this false teaching. The conclusion of the council was that the teaching that the Gentiles must be circumcised and keep the law to be saved was erroneous. (No one ever corrects the governing body of the Watchtower Society!)

The only instruction given to the Gentiles was "that they abstain from pollutions of idols, and from fornication, and from things strangled, and from blood" (Acts 15:20). But this was not some "new light" revealed to those gathered (as the J.W. governing body claims their new directives to be today), but was something written in the Old Testament (Lev. 17:13–15). Even when they gave this instruction to the Gentiles, they didn't write it as a command that had to be obeyed at the threat of being disfellowshipped, as the Watchtower governing body does today.

We find such a meeting only once in the Bible, and then it was not just the apostles but also the elders. The governing body of the Watchtower Society does not include the elders in their policy-making decisions. A central governing body which ruled over all the Christians cannot be found in the Bible. However, later on in Church history some leaders taught and practiced this. History teaches us that when all power came to rest in a man or group of men at the top, it caused the downfall of the church.

GOD

Biblical Christianity. There is one Triune God, eternally existing in three persons—Father, Son, and Holy Spirit. They are equal in power and glory and have the same attributes. One of His attributes is omnipresence. This means He is everywhere at the same time and is not confined to one location (1 Kings 8:27; Jer. 23:24). Some other attributes of God are omnipotence, omniscience, holiness, righteousness, mercifulness, faithfulness, longsuffering (patience), compassion, incorruptibility, consuming fire, graciousness, invisibility, immortality, etc.

Jehovah's Witnesses. According to their teachings, God (the Father) alone is eternal. He is the supreme power behind the universe. However, they claim that God has a finite form and is a spirit dwelling in a "spirit body."

They say that God is not omnipresent but is confined to one place because the Bible speaks of Him as having a location. On page 36 of the 1982 Watchtower publication *You Can Live Forever In Paradise On Earth,* it says:

> Since God is a person with a spiritual body, he must have a place to live. The Bible tells us that the heavens are God's "established *place* of dwelling." (1 Kings 8:43)

They used to teach that God dwelt on the star Alcyone in the constellation forming the Pleiades:

> The constellation of the seven stars forming the Pleiades appears to be the crowning center around which the known systems of the planets revolve even as our sun's planets obey the sun and travel in their respective orbits. It has been suggested, and with much weight, that one of the stars of that group is the dwelling-place of Jehovah. . . .

The constellation of the Pleiades is a small one compared with others which scientific instruments disclose to the wondering eyes of men. But the greatness in size of other stars or planets is small when compared with the Pleiades in importance, because the Pleiades is the place of the eternal throne of God. (*Reconciliation*, 1928, p. 14)

Some, however, believe that they have found the direction of it to be the Pleiades, and particularly Alcyone, the central one of the renowned Pleiadic stars. . . . Alcyone, then, as far as science has been able to perceive, would seem to be "the midnight throne" in which the whole system of gravitation has its central seat, and from which the Almighty governs his universe. (*Thy Kingdom Come* [*Studies in the Scriptures*, Vol. III], 1891, edition of 1903, p. 327)

Hardly any current Jehovah's Witness knows anything about this former teaching, but it does show how small they feel God is.

The Witnesses also teach that God is not omniscient (all-knowing). They say that if He were, then everything is "predestinated"—which would make God responsible for evil and the actions of all people. So they say that God chose to limit His knowledge of the future. God is compared to a human being who must exercise self-control and who can only function with a limited amount of foreknowledge.

They say God is both loving and vindictive. The vindictiveness of God is directed more toward Christendom (Roman Catholics, liberals, evangelicals, fundamentalists, all cults, etc.) than at the evils of the world. They stress that Christendom is corrupt and deserves the name "Babylon." However, they say very little about the anger, wrath, and judgment of God again sin.

Jehovah God does not play an important role in the Watchtower system. They teach that Jehovah God directly created only the Son. The Son is said to have created the universe and is now in control of it.

They teach that each day of creation was 7000 years long and not a literal twenty-four hours (*Insight on the Scriptures*, 1988, Vol. I, p. 545). Adam was created in the fall of 4026 B.C. at the end of the sixth day. They say that we are now in the seventh day of creation. Therefore, God has been resting during man's time on earth. The end of this present world is to come after 6000 years (which was to have happened in 1914, 1925, 1940, and 1975). The last 1000 years are to be the Millennium.

THE SON

Biblical Christianity.   He is the eternal Son of God, possesses all the attributes of the Godhead, is equal with the Father (Col. 2:9; John 5:18). He is truly God (Heb. 1:8–9) and not just an exalted angel (Heb. 1:5).

Jehovah's Witnesses.   They teach that the Son (also known as "The Word" or "Michael the archangel") was the first and only direct creation of Jehovah God and is called "God's representative." At first, the Son was only "a god"— not "a mighty god"—and was greatly inferior to the Father.

The Son's power to create the universe is said to have come from God through His holy spirit ("active force"). He was merely the "agent of instrumentality" through whom God worked. Jehovah's Witnesses place the Son in the same category as angels. It is important to remember that angels have their own personalities along with a certain amount of given power and knowledge.

The Son who lives in heaven has no relationship with or similarity to Jesus Christ who lived on this earth. They say that the Son willed himself out of existence when it came time for the man Jesus to be born on the earth. They use Philippians 2:7, "But made himself of no reputation," to try to prove this theory. Committing suicide is the only way that a person can annihilate himself (will himself out of existence). I understand the Bible to say that suicide is sin.

The Jehovah's Witnesses state this doctrine as fact without explaining it. If you ask for an explanation, they will say that it is a mystery. However, if you were to tell them that the Trinity is a mystery, they would not accept that as an answer.

JESUS CHRIST

Biblical Christianity. He humbled Himself in becoming a man (Phil. 2:5–8), but did not cease to be God. He was worshipped at the time of His birth (Heb. 1:6). His purpose in coming to earth was to reveal God and redeem sinful men (John 1:14,18; Matt. 1:21).

Jehovah's Witnesses. They teach that Jesus Christ was *only a man*. They say that neither the personality, the power, nor the knowledge of the annihilated Son existed in Jesus. They quote the beginning of John 1:14, "And the Word was made flesh," but ignore the rest of the verse which says, "and dwelt among us, (and we beheld his glory, the glory as of the only begotten of the Father,) full of grace and truth."

BIRTH OF CHRIST

Biblical Christianity. He was conceived by the Holy Spirit and born of the Virgin Mary (Isa. 7:14; Matt. 1:18,20,23; Luke 1:27).

Jehovah's Witnesses. They believe in the Virgin Birth though they deny the personality of the Holy Spirit. They say:

> Since actual conception took place, it appears that Jehovah God caused an ovum or egg cell in Mary's womb to become fertile, accomplishing this by transferal of the life of his firstborn Son from the spirit realm

to earth (Gal. 4:4). Only in this way could the child eventually born have retained identity as the same person who had resided in heaven as the Word. . . . From the results revealed in the Bible, it would appear that the perfect male life force (causing the conception) canceled out any imperfection existent in Mary's ovum, thereby producing a genetic pattern . . . that was perfect from its start. (*Aids to Bible Understanding*, p. 920)

It is difficult to understand how anyone can believe all that double-talk and fantasy.

RANK OF CHRIST

Biblical Christianity. From His birth He was the perfect God-man (1 Tim. 3:16) and the Christ (Luke 2:11).

Jehovah's Witnesses. They claim that Jesus Christ and Adam have the same rank. The only difference is that Adam sinned and Jesus did not. Jesus is supposed to have been no different from any other man until he reached the age of thirty. They say that Jesus was "the greatest man ever to walk this earth, the most outstanding figure of all human history" (*Yearbook*, 1983).

Jesus was not Christ until he was baptized the Christ at the age of thirty. The Jehovah's Witnesses claim that until Jesus was baptized he did not know that he had come to earth to die. This knowledge is supposed to have been gradually revealed to him after his anointing.

Jesus Christ was Jehovah's representative here on the earth. The Watchtower Society teaches that he had no power in himself. All the miracles and signs that he did were done by the power of God's active force. They teach that when Jesus Christ received worship and honor, he did so only as God's representative.

The Society uses the term "genetic transfer" to explain why Jesus was able to say that he came down from heaven though (according to their teachings) he was never in heaven. This term also allowed Jesus to claim to be "the only begotten Son of God" while the Son was non-existent at the time. In their vocabulary, "Son of Man" and "Son of God" have the same meaning. In the Christian's vocabulary, "Son of Man" refers to Christ's human nature, and "Son of God" refers to His divine nature.

The Jehovah's Witnesses use the term "Son of God" to refer to Jesus, Adam, the angels, and others. Jesus is one of many "sons of God." They feel that the greatest sin which a person can commit is to believe in the deity of Jesus Christ and in the Trinity, which they consider a "pagan" doctrine. The Society's main purpose is to tear down these doctrines.

DEATH OF JESUS

Biblical Christianity. Jesus Christ died for our sins, according to the Scripture, as a representative and substitutionary sacrifice. All who believe in Him are justified by His shed blood (1 Tim. 1:15; 2:6; 1 Cor. 15:3; Matt. 20:28; Eph. 1:7; 1 Pet. 1:18–19).

Jehovah's Witnesses. In an old Watchtower publication, *The Harp of God* (1921), they show Jesus hanging on a cross. Former Watchtower president J.F. Rutherford taught that Jesus died on a cross (*Reconciliation*, 1928, pp. 139, 199). Since then, their teaching has changed, and now they say Jesus died on a "torture stake." Current publications show Jesus on a single stake with His hands nailed above his head. One nail is used for both hands. This is contrary to Scripture which teaches, "Except I shall see in his hands the print of the nails, . . . I will not believe" (John 20:25).

Jesus is said to have given his life as a ransom only for those sins that we inherited from Adam. They say that the death of Christ assures that all mankind (except Jesus Christ himself and those disfellowshipped by the Watchtower Society) will come forth in the resurrection which, to them, is a re-creation. These resurrected ones will be given a second chance to come into subjection to God's government during the Millennium.

Since they say that Christ did not die for personal sins, the Witnesses do not talk about the forgiveness of these sins. Their main goal is to win the approval of Jehovah God by being in complete submission to the Watchtower Society. Loyalty to the Organization is synonymous with being loyal to Jehovah God. Since they claim that Jehovah God works through their organization only, all other religious organizations are members of "Babylon the Great." These are said to teach deceptively disguised doctrines of the devil.

The Society teaches that Christ was annihilated and his body disintegrated into gases within three days after his death. This annihilation was the end of Jesus, since they say that man's soul is not separate from his body. They teach that Jesus will not be resurrected with the rest of mankind because he would be "taking back the ransom price" if he were resurrected.

RESURRECTION

Biblical Christianity. Jesus Christ rose bodily from the dead (John 2:19–22; Matt. 28:6; Luke 24:33–43; 1 Cor. 15:4; Phil. 3:20–21).

Jehovah's Witnesses. They talk about "the resurrection of Jesus Christ" even though they say that Christ was completely annihilated after His death. They explain this "resurrection" by using parts of two verses. First Peter 3:18 says, "Being put to death in the flesh, but quickened by the Spirit." First Corinthians 15:44 says, "It is sown a natural body; it is raised a spiritual body." They take the "a" from 1 Corinthians and the "spirit" from 1 Peter, and say that Christ rose as "a spirit." They teach that this spirit is an angel which is the re-created Son (Michael).

As mentioned before, the Son in heaven ceased to exist

when Christ was conceived by Mary. Then once Jesus was annihilated, Jehovah God re-created the Son. For the Jehovah's Witnesses, all the references to the resurrection of Christ and his coming to life again refer to the re-created Son. Luke 24:36–43 proves this teaching to be false. The disciples "supposed that they had seen a spirit" (v. 37). Here we find "a spirit" like the words the Watchtower Society uses, but Jesus' reply is, "Behold my hands and my feet, that it is I myself: handle me, and see; for a spirit hath not flesh and bones, as ye see me have" (v. 39).

The only logical conclusion from the Society's explanation is that this re-created Michael-Son took the discarded body of Jesus and appeared in it, telling people that Jesus had risen from the dead. In other words, it was one of the greatest acts of imposture the world has ever known. What they are saying is that since Jesus told people that he was the annihilated "Son of God," then it was all right for the Son to say that he was the man Jesus Christ. The Society uses polite terms to cover up this revolting teaching.

The Society claims that the Son appeared to people in many different forms. They make this claim because, at times, the people did not recognize the Son when he appeared to them.

ASCENSION

Biblical Christianity. The Lord Jesus Christ ascended to heaven in His resurrected body and is now exalted at the right hand of God where, as our High Priest, He fulfills the ministry of Intercessor and Advocate (Acts 1:9–10; 7:56; Luke 24:50–51; Rom. 8:34; Eph. 4:8; 1 Pet. 3:22; 1 John 2:1).

Jehovah's Witnesses. They believe that physical bodies cannot enter heaven. Those who go to heaven are "spirit beings" in "spirit bodies." When Michael ascended to heaven, he discarded the body of Jesus as he entered the clouds. (This, of course, contradicts their teaching that the body was turned into gasses before Easter morning.)

They have added the title "Jesus Christ" to the other names that Michael is known by—"the Son" or "the Word." They mean Michael whenever they talk about Jesus being in heaven. When Michael was re-created and went back to heaven, he was given a more exalted position. He became "a mighty god" whereas before he was only "a god." They do not tell us what Michael did to deserve this promotion. When the Bible speaks about the exalted position of Jesus Christ (see Phil. 2:5–11), they say that it means Michael. He is also the Word that is King of kings and Lord of lords.

They believe that Christ (Michael) will reign in heaven for 1000 years. However, they also teach that the 144,000 re-created spirits will "co-reign" with him, giving the 144,000 equal power with Christ.

After the Millennium, Christ will be demoted from his exalted position and will turn over the kingdom to Jehovah God who has been resting for 7000 years. Since Christ finished everything, Jehovah God will continue to rest. They use 1 Corinthians 15:28 to try to prove this. It says, "And when all things shall be subdued unto him, then shall the Son also himself be subject unto him that put all things under him, that God may be all in all." They ignore the verses about Christ receiving an "everlasting kingdom" (Isa. 9:6–7), and do not realize that after the Millennium there will be no need for some of the distinctions between the members of the Trinity that we have today.

THE SECOND COMING

Biblical Christianity. Christians believe in the personal, imminent coming of the Lord Jesus Christ for His Church. After the Great Tribulation, He returns to earth to reign over the earth by establishing His millennial kingdom (Zech. 14:4–11; 1 Thess. 1:10; 4:13–18; 5:9; Rev. 3:10; 19:11–16; 20:1–6).

Jehovah's Witnesses. They have always emphasized the return of Christ and have set many dates as the time for his return. They do not believe that Jesus Christ will come in the clouds to call his saints to heaven before he sets up his millennial kingdom, but teach he will rule from heaven.

Russell said that in 1914 the world would end. Armageddon was to take place followed by the Millennium. When this did not happen, Russell revised the date to 1916 and then 1918. He did not want to admit that he was a false prophet.

J.F. Rutherford set 1925 as the year for Christ's return. Later he said that it would occur around 1940.

The Witnesses taught for a long time that the Millennium would begin before everyone who had been baptized into the Watchtower Society prior to 1914 died. Since people usually are seventeen years old before they are baptized, those still alive are in their nineties and are unlikely to live much longer. Since time is running out on the 1914 date, the latest "new light" states it is not those who were *baptized* before 1914, but those *born* before 1914.

They do not believe that Christ will come back physically to this earth. The Watchtower Society is to reign on earth under the direction of the 144,000.

SATAN

Biblical Christianity. Satan is an angel who had been one of the angels closest to God. He rebelled against Him in heaven. He is the author of sin and the cause of the fall. He is the open and declared enemy of God and man, and he shall be eternally punished in the Lake of Fire (Job 1:6–7; Isa. 14:12–17; Matt. 4:2–11; 25:41; Rev. 20:10).

Jehovah's Witnesses. In *The Truth that Leads to Eternal Life*, they tell us how a son of God became Satan.

So, the invisible spirit who later became the devil must at one time have been perfect, without defect as a creation of God, just like all the other millions of angelic "sons of God." (Job 38:7) How, then, did he go bad? After the creation of the first man and woman, this spirit creature entered on a course of rebellion against God. He developed a desire to be worshiped and so enticed Adam and Eve to rebel against God. (pp. 56–57)

The Society teaches that Satan received his power from the Father as did the other sons of God (including Jesus Christ). They do not tell us just how much of his power Satan can use since his defection. They claim that he is "a mighty spirit creature," "the god of this world," and that he has superhuman power. (We know that Satan has great power because he can duplicate some of God's works. A great struggle will take place when Satan is cast out of heaven.)

According to the Witnesses, Satan has this great power residing in himself. However, they imply that the Son does not have innate power, because they state that "The power for creation came from God through his holy spirit or active force." They also say that when Jesus was on earth, he could perform only through "the finger of God (God's active force)." Thus a reasonable conclusion is that Satan has more power than the firstborn Son of God and the earthly Lord Jesus Christ! They deny that, but if you study their teachings, you will reach the same conclusion.

THE 144,000

Biblical Christianity. We are now living in what is known as the Church Age, which began at Pentecost and will end when Christ returns in the clouds and calls His saints out of the world. At this time, God will take up His dealing with the nation of Israel again. Daniel 9:27 speaks about seven years of tribulation between the time Christ comes to take His saints out of the world and before He comes back and sets up His millennial kingdom upon this earth. This seven-year period is divided in two parts of three-and-one-half years each. The first half is known as the Tribulation and the latter half as the Great Tribulation. (Not all Christians agree on these details.)

It is generally believed that the 144,000 mentioned in Revelation 7:4-8 refers to a literal number of actual Jews (12,000 from each tribe except the tribe Dan), who are the faithful Jewish remnant saved during the Tribulation. Some believe that the 144,000 Jews will be the ones who preach the gospel to the ends of the earth during the Tribulation, but no one can be dogmatic on the subject. The calling-out and the work of the 144,000 is something that is still future. It is very certain that these 144,000 come out of the Great Tribulation (Rev. 7:14) along with the great multitude who are found in Revelation 7:9-17. The Bible says that Christ's saints will live and reign with Him for 1000 years, but it never limits the number of saints (Rev. 3:21; 20:4-6).

Jehovah's Witnesses. They believe that only 144,000 people have been chosen to go to heaven and reign with Christ for 1000 years. They say the 144,000 make up the Bride of Christ and are called "The Bride Class," "The Little Flock," "The John Class," or "The Anointed Ones." They are also known as the "Kingdom" or the "Faithful and Discreet Slave" class. J.W.'s say that the selection of the 144,000 began when Christ chose his disciples and has continued down through time until 1935—when the Society announced that the number was complete.

When the Watchtower Society began, they taught that all its members would be part of the 144,000 who would go to heaven. These people did not have to be more spiritual than the average person; they just had to join the Society. One of the supposed benefits of being a Jehovah's Witness was the assurance of going to heaven.

However, when membership in the Society approached 144,000, they realized that they had a problem. In 1935, they said that the 144,000 was complete. Once this happened, the

Society had to change its teaching on the future state of man. The Society now teaches that those who will live on the "new earth" (or paradise) are the fortunate ones because they can live as families. The 144,000 must give up the pleasures of the new earth in order to reign with Christ. Very few Witnesses want to make this sacrifice. The wife of a Jehovah's Witness missionary said to me, "I have *no* desire to go to heaven."

Charles Russell, however, taught that the Millennium began when Christ's reign started in heaven in 1874. The members of the 144,000 who died before that time were then resurrected as "spirit persons" in "spirit bodies" and began to reign with Christ. Since then, the anointed ones go directly to heaven when they die.

THE GREAT CROWD (Rev. 7:9) or THE OTHER SHEEP (John 10:16)

Biblical Christianity. The "other sheep" are those who were not of the Jewish fold at the time Jesus was speaking, but are Gentiles who in the future (after His death on the cross) would believe on Him. As the end of John 10:16 clearly states, "there shall be one fold, and one shepherd." (See Isa. 56:8; Ezek. 34:23; 37:24; John 11:52; 17:20; Eph. 2:11–19.) The "great multitude" in Revelation 7:9 are those who "come out of the Great Tribulation," as clearly stated in verse 14. The Bible never divides believers into two classes, one superior to the other.

Jehovah's Witnesses. They divide themselves into two classes. The first group is the "anointed ones" discussed under "The 144,000." As of 1994, 8,500 Jehovah's Witnesses claim to be of this class. All were members of the Society before 1935. All the members of the governing body have to be of this class.

The remainder of the Witnesses are in the "great crowd" class (from Revelation 7:9). All Jehovah's Witnesses living today expect to survive the battle of Armageddon and inhabit the paradise on earth which they will prepare during the millennial reign of Christ. The "new earth" will be the immediate reward earned by the great crowd because of their loyalty to Jehovah God. They will earn their reward through their present preaching activities (door-to-door selling of Watchtower publications).

ARMAGEDDON (Rev. 16:16; 19:17–20:3)

Biblical Christianity. Armageddon (mentioned by this name only in Revelation 16:16) is the hill and valley of Megiddo, west of the Jordan in the plain of Jezreel, between Samaria and Galilee in the land of Palestine. This is the appointed place for the great battle which will occur after the Tribulation, just before Christ sets up His millennial kingdom. The armies of the beast and false prophet will be destroyed at Christ's descending to earth in glory (Rev. 19:11, 15, 19, 21). It may be more than just a local battle because of the immensity of the armies that are involved—over two hundred million (Rev. 9:13–18; 16:12–14).

Jehovah's Witnesses. They teach that before the millennial reign begins on earth, a time of great destruction will occur because of the battle of Armageddon. They declare that only members of the Watchtower Society will survive this nuclear holocaust. They use this teaching as a proselytizing tool, telling people that they need to join the Society so they will not be killed.

They believe that Armageddon will be caused by a confrontation between the King of the North (supposedly the Soviet Union) and the King of the South (the United States). They teach that nuclear weapons will be used, but the battle will be directed by God so as to protect the Jehovah's Witnesses. (For details see the Watchtower publication *United in Worship of the Only True God*, 1983, pp. 182–3.)

They say that the first thing to be destroyed will be all the world's religions (except the Watchtower Society, of course). This destruction of other religions is one of their favorite teachings. In the book *Make Sure of All Things*, Armageddon is said to be: "The battle of Jehovah God Almighty in which his executive officer, Jesus Christ, leads invisible forces of righteousness to destroy Satan and his demonic and human organization, eliminating wickedness from the universe and vindicating Jehovah's universal sovereignty" (1953, p. 24).

In *From Paradise Lost to Paradise Regained* (1958, pp. 203–4, 207–11), they give a lengthy description of what happens at the battle of Armageddon: how the enemies of God will be killed; how their bodies will be devoured by worms, birds, and beasts; and how for seven months the Armageddon survivors will gather up and bury the bones.

This same Watchtower publication shows pictures of skyscrapers falling over (apparently from an earthquake), people in water drowning, hailstones hitting and killing people, buildings on fire, and the earth opening up and people falling into a giant hole. The logical conclusion from these pictures is that most buildings will be destroyed, along with all roads and other means of transportation.

Remember, it is only the "lucky" Jehovah's Witnesses who get to survive all this awful destruction—and then have to begin to build "paradise."

THE NEW EARTH

Biblical Christianity. The Bible refers to the new heavens and new earth four times (Isa. 65:17; 66:22; 2 Pet. 3:13; Rev. 21:1). It is believed that this new earth refers to the time when Christ reigns for 1000 years upon the earth, though it might continue beyond this time. Christ will reign in righteousness over the earth, but only a few details are given about the actual conditions on the new earth. Isaiah 35:1 says: ". . . and the desert shall rejoice, and blossom as the rose." Another reference is in Isaiah 65:18–25, where it says that the span of life will be greatly lengthened and animals will become tame. There has been much speculation about the new earth which is not biblically based. One thing is certain—no born-again Christian living today will go directly into the new earth because each believer will be taken to heaven before it is established (1 Thess. 4:13–18). Revelation 20:4 says that "they lived and reigned with Christ a thousand years," but what relationship we will have to the new earth is not explained.

Many groups (the Jehovah's Witnesses and others) make the mistake of associating paradise with the new earth. The two are not the same. The Bible clearly teaches that paradise is heaven and not the new earth. In 2 Corinthians 12:2 Paul speaks about being "caught up to the third heaven." Then in verse 4 he says, "he was caught up into paradise." Clearly heaven and paradise are the same place. Revelation 2:7 says, "To him that overcometh will I give to eat of the tree of life, which is in the midst of the paradise of God." In Revelation 22 a description of heaven is given and the tree of life is mentioned three times, in verses 2, 14, and 19, which clearly shows that paradise is synonymous with heaven.

Jehovah's Witnesses. They teach that following Armageddon this earth will become a paradise like the earth was before Adam's fall. Their books picture people living in beautiful houses with lakes and snow-capped mountains in the background. But this does not happen immediately after Armageddon. This must be accomplished by the Jehovah's Witnesses who, they claim, will survive Armageddon. However, the task will not be fully completed until sometime after the 1000-year reign of Christ.

The rebuilding of this whole earth by four million Jehovah's Witnesses after the awful destruction at Armageddon will be a mammoth job. They estimate that the clean-up operation will take about one hundred years. Of course, the immediate task will be to dispose of the five billion bodies. The survivors first will have to wait around until the worms, beasts, and birds eat the bodies. (What a delightful thought.) Next they must dispose of all the skeletons. After this gruesome job is over, they must remove all the damage caused by the nuclear bombs, fires, earthquakes, etc., before the rebuilding can begin. This work will have to be started by using primitive hand tools, requiring a lot of hard manual labor, since all mechanized equipment will have been destroyed. Land also must be readied for farming, since they assert that everyone will have his own garden.

Though the Watchtower publications give some indication of what must be done to build paradise upon this planet, most of the Witnesses have never thought through the details—some of which are found in *From Paradise Lost to Paradise Regained.*

> The first thing that the people who live through Armageddon must do is to tear down the ruins that will be left upon the earth. They must clean out everything that is part of Satan's wrongdoing. . . .
>
> Then they must build up good things to replace what was destroyed. Everyone who lives through Armageddon will have a part in this good work. Paradise will be spread earth-wide. The whole earth will be made into a garden. This will be a happy work. Every person will be making something good and useful. No one will be working for another man. Each person will enjoy the results of his own labor, and the work of his own hands.
>
> . . . then there will be no hunger, no lack of work, no famines, no dreaded water shortages and no unlawful market places where men take advantage of the poor. . . .
>
> With everyone who lives obeying Jehovah, there will be no crime, no misdoing, no lawlessness. . . .
>
> Even more, you will have good health so that you can enjoy life in Paradise. You will not be sick or in pain. . .
>
> . . . healthy children will be born then. . . . (pp. 220–3)

However, the Jehovah's Witnesses are not building this paradise just for themselves. They believe that most of the people who have ever lived will be resurrected. At least for a while—one hundred to five hundred years—these multitudes can enjoy the hard labor of the Jehovah's Witnesses. The Watchtower Society estimates that twenty billion people have lived on earth since the world was created. One hundred years after the battle of Armageddon, they say, God might re-create three percent of those who have died. Over the next five hundred years, the rest of the people will gradually be re-created. During this time, the four million Witnesses (and the new arrivals) must continue to build houses and make furniture, appliances, and clothing for the people as they are re-created. (They give more detail concerning this in the Watchtower publication *Insight on the Scriptures*, 1988, Vol. II, pp. 792–3.)

It seems to me that it would be a curse rather than a blessing to survive Armageddon. Remember, the Society teaches that death is like falling asleep with no pain. They declare that Armageddon occurs because people are so wicked. Yet the wicked are said to die a painless death and will be in a state of unconsciousness in the grave while the four million Witnesses clean up the mess left by Armageddon. The god of the Watchtower Society seems to be much kinder to the wicked than he is to the Jehovah's Witnesses. I would not want to be on earth inhaling the stench of the dead bodies and watching billions of worms eating them up!

SECOND CHANCE

Biblical Christianity. The Bible never states anywhere that there will be a "second chance" after death. Hebrews 9:27 says, "And as it is appointed unto men once to die, but after this the judgment. . . ." If there were a second chance and people failed that test, then they would have to die physically twice, which violates Scripture. The Bible only speaks of two resurrections—which are separated by 1000 years. John 5:28–29 says, "Marvel not at this: for the hour is coming, in the which all that are in the grave shall hear his voice, and shall come forth; they that have done good, unto the resurrection of life; and they that have done evil, unto the resurrection of damnation." The resurrection of life takes place for those who have been born again before the millennial reign of Christ (1 Thess. 4:13–18; Rev. 20:4–6) and the resurrection of damnation occurs at the end of the 1000-year reign of Christ. If people fail to respond to the gospel of Christ in this life, there will not be a second chance in the next.

Jehovah's Witnesses. During the Millennium just about all mankind will be resurrected from the state of unconsciousness and given a second chance to come into conformity to God's will—by which they mean, become a Jehovah's Witness.

Included in the earthly resurrection will be (1) the faithful witnesses of Jehovah who died before Christ did, (2) the billions of other people who will be brought back in the "resurrection of judgment" and (3) the people of good will who today take their stand on God's side but who through sickness, old age or another cause happen to die before Armageddon is fought.

It is thought that the earthly resurrection will be spread out over a period of time so that all these people after being resurrected on earth can be taken care of in an orderly way, and without confusion. The people brought back earlier will help to get things ready for the others who are yet to return. (*From Paradise Lost to Paradise Regained*, p. 232)

The Watchtower Society teaches that Jesus Christ died for the sin nature that we inherited from Adam, not for our personal sins. Since Christ took care of Adam's sin, they claim that everyone except Jesus Christ Himself, disfellowshipped and disassociated Jehovah's Witnesses, and a

.few undetermined others, will be resurrected. However, they do not teach that the actual body that went into the grave will be resurrected—just someone with identical personality and knowledge. This personality and knowledge has been stored in God's memory. They say that God will re-create an independent human body as it pleases Him, but it will be recognizable by their acquaintances and have the same personality as the person they look like. In their own words, they assert:

> Those who come back to life on earth will not come from Hades or the grave perfect in the flesh. Through Jesus Christ who died for them God will create new bodies for them. Although God creates these, yet they will not be perfect human bodies. Why not? Because those bodies must match the personalities and powers of mind of the people who are resurrected. Their personalities and powers of mind were not perfect or sinless when they died. So their new bodies must match the kind of persons they are when resurrected. (*Ibid.*, p. 234)

The Society uses the first part of Romans 6:23—"For the wages of sin is death"—and teaches at a person pays for his personal sins when he dies. The price is the same for everybody regardless of how much they have sinned. Because a person has paid for his sins by dying, he will have a clean record when he is re-created during the Millennium. (I have not been able to find out how those who survive Armageddon will pay for *their* sins, since they have not died!)

The Society teaches that a Jehovah's Witness has his personality changed here on earth. Because of this change, he will automatically conform to Jehovah's will when he is re-created. Those who are not Jehovah's Witnesses before death will need to be educated in Jehovah's ways on the new earth. J.W.'s believe that those who have been faithful Witnesses will be given the job of teaching those people how to be loyal to Jehovah and Christ. They believe this education process with take from one hundred to five hundred years.

However, Paradise will not be a perfect place because people will still be able to choose to do wrong. This is confirmed by their publication which says:

> These people will be brought back into the paradise earth. They will be taught the truth. They will be shown what is right. Then they will be judged according to what they do about it. If they obey God's commands they will get life. If they do not obey God's commands they will go into everlasting death, just as Adam did after he deliberately disobeyed God. (*Ibid.*, p. 229)
>
> When "death and Hades" have been destroyed, the only thing that would then cause a person to lose his life would be his own willful rebellion against God. (*Ibid.*, p. 234)
>
> Those who come forth to a "resurrection of judgment" will be judged during the thousand years of Christ's reign. Everyone who is alive on earth will receive great blessings during that time, but some resurrected for judgment, or some who are born as children to the people who live through Armageddon, still may refuse to serve God. Anyone who refuses to obey God's kingdom after a long-enough trial will be put to death. His death could not be blamed on anyone else, but would be only because he had willfully refused to obey God. Such a one is sentenced to destruction before the end of the thousand-year reign of Christ Jesus. (*Ibid.*, p. 237)
>
> So after being given full opportunity to change their ways and to learn righteousness, such wicked ones will be destroyed. Some will be put to death even before Judgment Day ends. (Isaiah 65:20) They will not be permitted to remain to corrupt or spoil the paradise earth. (*You Can Live Forever in Paradise on Earth*, p. 178)

The fact that some people will be annihilated during the Millennium creates a major problem. It means that this paradise will *not* be a perfect place in which to live, and there will be more bodies to dispose of. Yet they teach that no one will ever be sick or grow old and die; in fact, they teach that the old will even grow young again! But if people will be destroyed during this time, how will it be done? The only possible way I know is that God must strike the person dead. Then someone must get rid of the body. But the Witnesses teach that there will be no funeral parlors and thus no undertakers. So, it seems, the beautiful yards of some people will have to be dug up for graves!

FINAL TEST

Biblical Christianity. At the end of the 1000-year reign of Christ on the earth (the Millennium), Satan will be released for a short time (Rev. 20:3, 7-8). He will gather a great army and fight against Christ. However, he is defeated (Rev. 20:9-10) and cast in the lake of fire. The Bible does not tell us where Satan gets all the people who follow him, but it is generally believed that there will be children born to those who are on the earth during the millennial reign of Christ who will be in subjection to Christ outwardly and not inwardly. When Satan is released, these will follow him in rebellion to Christ. This does not involve any Christian living today, because they will be in heaven and will be eternally kept by the power of God.

Jehovah's Witnesses. They maintain that even after mankind has attained perfection and paradise has been restored, people must pass a final test before God will consider them to be living or have "everlasting life." This test is to occur at the end of the Millennium. Again quoting from *From Paradise Lost to Paradise Regained*:

Everyone who is alive anywhere on earth must

face this last test, even the princes of the "new earth" and the sheeplike people who lived through Armageddon. Everyone on earth will be judged according to how he meets this test.

"How will the last test come about?" The final test will come when Satan and his demons who were bound and imprisoned in the abyss at Armageddon, will be let out for a little while. . . .

Satan's heart will not have changed. Again he will try to turn all men away from God. He will use some kind of selfishness as his weapon. He will try to make people think that they will be better off if they follow him than they would be if they did right and obeyed God. . . . So Satan will use some sly appeal to selfishness at the end of the thousand years. But whatever method he uses, he will do all that he can to take everyone into final destruction with him. (pp. 238–9)

This quotation speaks about Satan being "bound and imprisoned in the abyss at Armageddon"; but they do not believe that this was a place of punishment. They teach that Satan is to be annihilated—in a state of unconsciousness—for 1000 years and then re-created. They further declare that Satan will be destroyed again after he is left free to deceive people for a short while. However, to them destruction means only that once again he will be annihilated—in a state of unconsciousness.

The Society does not say how many people will not pass the final test, but they suggest that many will not. But no matter the number, we see that the paradise created by the Watchtower Society will be filled again with many dead bodies that must be gotten rid of.

Again in the book *From Paradise Lost to Paradise Regained*, in a chapter titled "The Last Judgment of Mankind," they write:

Now what have we learned about judgment? We

have learned that a person could fall away and be judged unfavorably either now or at Armageddon, or during the thousand years of Christ's reign, or at the end of the final test. (p. 241)

No Jehovah's Witness can have assurance of an eternal future until he passes the final test. What an agony it must be to have a religion that cannot offer assurance!

HEAVEN

Biblical Christianity. All who have put their faith and trust in the Lord Jesus Christ as their personal Savior will go to heaven when they die (1 Pet. 1:4–5; 2 Tim. 4:18; 1 Cor. 5:1–2; 1 John 5:13). Jesus revealed that heaven was a wonderful place (John 14:1–3), and He prayed that all believers would see His glory in heaven (John 17:24). Heaven is a perfect place where believers will be in perfect fellowship with God (Rev. 21:1–4). No sin can enter heaven (Rev. 21:27).

Jehovah's Witnesses. Strange as it may seem, this is one teaching that they don't say too much about. They promised all the early Witnesses a place in heaven, but after the 144,000 openings were filled (which they claim happened in 1935), they had to change their teaching on heaven.

Now they teach that those who go to heaven must make a great sacrifice because they will not be given bodies and cannot live with their loved ones. Current Witnesses have no desire to go to heaven.

The June 1, 1981, issue of *The Watchtower* magazine asked,

And what is this? Bliss in heaven sprawled out on the billowy cloud, twanging a harp as you float along in space and eternity? No! It is not that vain and useless existence that idle dreamers have conjured upon as heavenly life.

SIN

Biblical Christianity. Man was created in the image and likeness of God, but when Adam rebelled against God he took on a sin nature and this sin nature has been passed on to all humans so that all are born with an inherited sin nature. Man has chosen to sin, so he is also a sinner by choice and responsible for his sin. Sin is anything that is in direct violation of the will of God (Ps. 51:5; 58:3; Isa. 53:6; 64:6; Jer. 17:9; Rom. 1:24–32; 1 Tim. 1:5).

If a religious group is off on the biblical doctrine of sin, like the Jehovah's Witnesses, they will be off on all their other doctrines. If they understand the biblical doctrine of sin, then Christ will be presented as the only way of salvation.

Jehovah's Witnesses. They do not believe that man is basically sinful. (Their idea is similar to the Buddhist idea of sin, which teaches that man is basically good but has collected some dust. This dust can be cleared away by one's own effort.) The Watchtower Society teaches that when we are born we are tainted with Adam's sin, but sin is more of a moral failure than evil coming from a sinful nature and being a deliberate act of rebellion against God. The reason we do bad things, they say, is because we allow Satan to tempt us; so it is due more to Satan's influence than to our nature. (One of their missionaries in Nagoya, Japan, told me that he did not know of any sin that a person could commit that would make him worthy of hell. Another Witness once said to me, "If Jesus Christ was truly God, then the sacrifice was too great." In other words, man is not that great of a sinner so as to need God to pay for his sins.)

They liken sin to being out of harmony with God's standards of conduct, but we are not really responsible for this because we don't know God's will by nature. Thus, instead of needing forgiveness because of a sinful nature which causes willful sin, people need to be educated to know

God's standards. They teach that this education process is accomplished by "taking in accurate knowledge" of God through studying Watchtower publications and being in harmony with (complete submission to) God's organization, the Watchtower Society. (The worst sin a Witness can commit is to not be in total subjection to the Organization.) Therefore, salvation is a process, and not a once-for-all act of trusting Jesus Christ as one's personal Savior. Of course, a Jehovah's Witness can never know if he has taken in *enough* accurate knowledge. Another major problem is that the "accurate knowledge" of the Watchtower Society always keeps changing, so a Witness continually has to keep taking in more knowledge (forgetting the previous) and always changing his actions.

IMMORTALITY OF THE SOUL

Biblical Christianity. Man is made up of body, soul, and spirit (1 Thess. 5:23). The soul continues on in a conscious state when separated from the body at the time of death (Gen. 35:18–19; 1 Kings 17:21–22; Matt. 10:28; Rev. 6:9–11). At the time of the resurrection it will again be united with the body and the saved will go into heaven (1 Thess. 4:13–18), but the unsaved will be cast into the lake of fire for eternity (Rev. 20:11–15).

Jehovah's Witnesses. They believe that the soul and body are *one* and cannot be separated. When the body dies, the soul dies.

The soul is not in any way synonymous with "spirit." The spirit means "breath of life from God" or "life force." It does not have a personality, nor can it think speak, hear, see, or feel. It does not have a separate existence after death. For the Witnesses, "the dead are dead and there is no survival after death."

The Society does not explain how the 144,000 will exist in heaven without a human body. They say that the 144,000 are clothed in "spiritual bodies." Yet they teach that a physical body is necessary for existence. According to the Society, if there is no physical body, there is no soul. How, then, can they exist in the next life without a soul?

SALVATION

Biblical Christianity.   Salvation is the gift of God brought to man by grace and received by personal faith in the Lord Jesus Christ, whose precious blood was shed on Calvary for our sins so that we might be forgiven (Eph. 2:8–9; John 1:12; Eph. 1:7; 1 Pet. 1:18–19).

Jehovah's Witnesses.   For them salvation comes through works done for the Watchtower Society instead of through faith in Jesus Christ. Membership in the Society follows baptism by immersion. The Witness must be diligent in distributing Watchtower literature from door to door. Every active Witness performs this "preaching" work. They divide them into three groups:

PUBLISHERS—Each publisher is expected to record a minimum of one hour per month in door-to-door service. Good Witnesses are actually supposed to reach the quota of ten hours per month.

PIONEERS—Each pioneer is expected to spend ninety hours per month in door-to-door service. Pioneer helpers are ones who can't spend ninety hours per month but who do give a lot more than ten hours per month.

SPECIAL PIONEERS—Those who spend 140 hours per month in door-to-door service.

Each person keeps careful records of the time he spends "preaching." As long as one stays in the good graces of the Society, his record will be kept on file. If there is a falling-out with the Society, the records will be destroyed, and he is said to have earned no merit before God.

Jehovah's Witnesses must conform to the dictates of the Watchtower Society because the Society claims to represent

God's will on earth. To rebel against the organization is to invite obliteration. In order to gain eternal life, a Witness must not waste time and energy pursuing the materialistic pleasures of the world. For this reason, few obtain a college education or a responsible job. Instead, they use their time to preach the news of Jehovah's Kingdom. Nonconformity to the will of the Society brings severe social censure which: (1) Brings separation from their friends and relatives; (2) Keeps the Witness from entering Paradise.

Since the Witnesses teach that salvation is a process and not a completed act, they can't be certain of obtaining it. Using 1 Corinthians 9:24–27, Hebrews 6:4–8, and 2 Peter 2:21–22, they teach that it is possible to fall away. This falling away is apparently a very real possibility, because from 1970 to 1980 one-third of the Witnesses were disfellowshipped or disassociated themselves from the movement.

The Society talks about Jesus being "Savior" and "Redeemer," but he plays no part in their salvation. According to their beliefs, Christ gave his life so that mankind might be resurrected and given another chance on the new earth. If you ask a Jehovah's Witness what Christ did for him personally, he might say that Christ died for his past sins, meaning those he inherited from Adam.

HELL

Biblical Christianity. The souls of unbelievers remain, after death, in conscious misery until the second resurrection when, with soul and body reunited, they shall appear at the Great White Throne judgment and shall be cast into the Lake of Fire, where they shall suffer everlasting conscious punishment. (See Luke 16:19–26; Matt. 25:41–46; Mark 9:43–48; 2 Thess. 1:7–9; Jude 6–7; Rev. 20:11–15.)

Jehovah's Witnesses. They teach that there will not be any kind of punishment after death. They say that hell is "mankind's common grave." They teach that people are annihilated at the time of death and that they enter a state of complete unconsciousness. They remain in this state until the time they are re-created during the Millennium. However, all will not be re-created at the same time; this will take place over a five-hundred-year period. They claim that Jehovah's Witnesses can ask Jehovah God to re-create their non-Witness relatives first so that they will have the first chance to be taught the Watchtower doctrines.

SCRIPTURE

Biblical Christianity. The Holy Scriptures of the Old and New Testament are the verbally inspired Word of God, the final authority for faith and life, inerrant in the original writings, infallible and God-breathed (2 Tim. 3:16–17; 2 Pet. 1:20–21; Matt. 5:18; John 16:12–13). The Bible does not need to be illuminated by any special group of men or an organization, nor is education a special key to understanding it. The Holy Spirit is the one who leads a person into the truth of God's Word. The Christian should test all religious books, organizations and speakers through the Bible, and not interpret the Bible by what religious books, organizations and speakers say about it.

Jehovah's Witnesses. They too say that the entire Bible is inspired of God and that they believe all of it. However, they have a much different idea of "inspiration" than most Bible-believing Christians and do not believe in the verbal inspiration of Scripture. They teach that the authors of the Bible were only inspired in their basic "idea" or "thought," and then each writer put these ideas into his own words. They teach that the Bible cannot be taken literally, but must be "illuminated" by the Watchtower Society. In the early days, Charles Russell was the only one who could illuminate the Bible. The next two presidents continued this practice.

They teach that inspiration comes directly from God through their organization. They do not believe the Bible as

God has written it. In fact, many of their teachings are contrary to the Bible.

Bible study to them means an examination of Watchtower literature under the guidance of a Jehovah's Witness. They talk about reading the Bible, but in reality they do not read much of it. In fact, they are almost forbidden to read it on their own. (One district overseer who had been a Witness for over twenty years had not read the Bible through twice. The most that any Witness that I have talked to has read the Bible through is four times.) Official Watchtower publications must be used in every Bible study.

They teach that only a small portion of the Bible was written for the average Jehovah's Witness. Most of the Bible is said to be written only for the anointed class (the 144,000). The average Witness feels that he has no reason to read the Bible when most of it is not written for him and what is written for him can only be interpreted by the Society. The Watchtower Society's attitude toward individual Bible reading and study is shown by the following quotes:

> Thus, the one who doubts to the point of becoming an apostate sets himself up as a judge. He thinks he knows better than his fellow Christians, but also than the "faithful and discreet slave" through whom he has learned the best part, if not all that he knows about Jehovah God and his purposes. He develops a spirit of independency, and becomes "proud in heart . . . something detestable to Jehovah" (Proverbs 16:14). Some apostates even think they know better than God, as regards his ordering the events in the outworking of his purposes. Two other causes of apostasy are therefore ingratitude and presumption (2 Peter 2:10b–13a). (*The Watchtower*, August 1, 1980, pp. 19–20)

"Faithful and discreet slave" is a term that Witnesses use to refer to the Watchtower organization. It is okay for the leaders to be proud and have the attitude that they know everything, but they don't want others to read the Bible and get ideas that do not agree with theirs.

> To be an example in speaking, Christian under-shepherds must not go "beyond the things that are written" (1 Corinthians 4:6). Whether in matters of doctrine, morals, or Christian organization, an overseer should "preach the word" (2 Timothy 4:2). If he were to introduce strictly personal opinions or to spread ideas contrary to the teaching received through the "FAITHFUL AND DISCREET SLAVE," this would cause confusion. Rather than pushing ahead presumptuously in a course that would lead to dishonor, therefore, why not wait upon Jehovah and his organization (Proverbs 11:2)? Perhaps there will be further explanation or clarification on the subject later. Or, through prayer and diligent study of God's Word with the help of the Watchtower publications, the elder may find that he was wrong and will be glad that he did not spread his mistaken views. (*The Watchtower*, September 1, 1980, p. 23)
>
> We all need help to understand the Bible and we cannot find the scriptural guidance we need outside the "faithful and discreet slave" organization. (*The Watchtower*, February 15, 1981, p. 19)

When they quote 1 Corinthians 4:6, "Do not go beyond the things that are written" (NWT), they mean what the Watchtower Society teaches.

The Society claims that the religion approved by Jehovah God must conform in all parts to the Bible. Yet they know that if their people began to study the Bible, they would discover that the beliefs of the Society do not conform to the Bible in all parts.

When Charles Russell got some ideas, he went to the Bible to find verses that he felt would prove his ideas. This practice has continued ever since. They completely ignore the context and often only use one or two words from a verse. Once they find a few verses that they feel prove their doctrine, they say that all other verses in the Bible concerning that doctrine must conform to their ideas.

For example: They deny the deity of Jesus Christ and use John 14:28b, John 20:17b, and Mark 13:32 to "prove" that they are right.

• John 14:28b says, "For my Father is greater than I."

• John 20:17b says, "I ascend unto my Father, and your Father; and to my God, and your God." They say that if Jesus had a God, then he could not be God.

• Mark 13:32 says, "But of that day and that hour knoweth no man, no, not the angels which are in heaven, neither the Son, but the Father." They say that if Jesus was God He would know everything. However, Jesus was speaking here from His human nature and not His divine nature. (It is interesting to note that the God of the Watchtower does not know everything. They state that if God knew everything He would be the author of sin; thus He has voluntarily chosen not to know everything. But this undermines their interpretation of Mark 13:32.)

Since these three verses "prove" that Jesus is not God, they say that all other Scripture concerning the deity of Christ must be interpreted in the light of these verses. If they would acknowledge that Jesus was both man and God, they would not have this problem.

Though the Watchtower Society claims to be the only representative of Jehovah on earth, and though they insist that all illumination comes directly from God through their organization, they keep changing their doctrines and teachings. They try to justify this by using Proverbs 4:18 which says, "But the path of the just is as the shinning light, that shineth more and more unto the perfect day." They say that God is continually giving "new light."

The Society compares this to science. They say that as man is always making advances in science and having to change the former teachings in science, so man is also making advances in the understanding of the Bible. The problem with this is that the understanding of science has come from men who are not omniscient, while their "light" on the Bible is said to come from Jehovah God who *is* omniscient. Because God is omniscient, He should not have to keep changing His teachings.

Because the teachings of the Society change so often, a person has to keep changing his beliefs or be called an apostate for clinging to the old ideas. It is impossible for them ever to say that what they are teaching at a given moment is absolutely true. They have to continue changing their doctrines as their false interpretations are uncovered.

The Watchtower Society developed its own translation of the Bible (the New World Translation, or NWT) because other translations contradicted their teachings. Therefore, when it comes to the doctrines which they deny (deity of Christ, Trinity, etc.), they deliberately change the text to conform to their beliefs. They now call the other translations "the devil's Bible."

A Jehovah's Witness will seem to know the Bible and will have many verses memorized. But don't be deceived; he has only memorized the verses they taught him and knows very little about the rest of the Bible. The Watchtower Society uses only six percent of the Bible in its publications.

THE HOLY SPIRIT

Biblical Christianity. The Holy Spirit is a person and is rightly called God (Acts 5:3–4). He convicts the world of sin, of righteousness, and of judgment. He is the Supernatural Agent in regeneration, baptizing all believers into the body of Christ, indwelling and sealing them unto the day of redemption (John 16:8–11; 2 Cor. 3:6; 1 Cor. 12:12–14; Rom. 8:9; Eph. 1:13–14). He is the Divine Teacher who guides believers into all truth (John 16:13). Along with the ascended Jesus, He gives various gifts to believers (Eph. 4:8; 1 Cor. 8–11).

Jehovah's Witnesses. They deny the personality of the Holy Spirit; they speak of Him as "God's active force," but they cannot tell you what that means. They desperately use every means they can to try to convince people that the Holy Spirit is not the third Person in the Godhead. Some quotes from the Watchtower publication *Insight on the Scriptures* (one of the standard works on their beliefs) reveal to what extent they will go in order to try to convince people of their unbiblical position.

> **Personification does not prove personality.** It is true that Jesus spoke of the holy spirit as a "helper" and spoke of such a helper as "teaching," "bearing witness," "giving evidence," "guiding," "speaking," "hearing," and "receiving." In so doing, the original Greek shows Jesus at times applying the personal pronoun "he" to that "helper." . . . However, it is not unusual in the Scriptures for something that is not actually a person to be personalized or personified. . . .
> **Lacks personal identification.** Since God himself is a Spirit and is holy and since all his faithful angelic sons are spirits and are holy, it is evident that if the "holy spirit" were a person, there should reasonably be given some means in the Scriptures to distinguish and identify such spirit person from all these other "holy spirits." It would be expected that, at the very least, the definite article would be used with it in all cases where it is not called "God's holy spirit" or is not modified by some similar expression. This would at least distinguish it as THE Holy Spirit. But, on the contrary, in a large number of cases the expression "holy spirit" appears in the original Greek without the article, thus indicating its lack of personality. (Vol. II, p. 1019)

They then list twenty-one places in the Greek New Testament where "the" is not found before "Holy Spirit.

However, the Watchtower publications are to be read,

not investigated. I went through the New World Translation of the Bible and found one hundred and eight places where "the" *is* found before "Spirit" and "Holy Spirit." The definite article "the" is found in some of the most important verses on the Holy Spirit *in their own translation.* For instance:

• Matthew 12:31–32, where it speaks about "blasphemy against the spirit" and "whoever speaks against the holy spirit."

• Matthew 28:19, "Go therefore and make disciples of people of all the nations, baptizing them in the name of the Father and of the Son and of the holy spirit."

• John 14:26, "But the helper, the holy spirit. . . ."

• Acts 5:3, "Ananias, why has Satan emboldened you to play false to the holy spirit. . . ?"

• Acts 13:2, ". . . the holy spirit said. . . ."

• 2 Corinthians 13:14, "The undeserved kindness of the Lord Jesus Christ and the love of God and the sharing in the holy spirit be with all of you."

Another Watchtower quote likens the Holy Spirit to an electric current:

Variety of operations. Even as an electric current can be used to accomplish a tremendous variety of things, so God's spirit is used to commission and enable persons to do a wide variety of things. (*Insight on the Scriptures,* p. 1021)

The Watchtower Society, like many other groups, does not deny the personality of the Holy Spirit because of the lack of biblical evidence, but because they have no need for Him. They do not believe that they are very bad sinners, so they do not need the convicting power of the Holy Spirit for salvation nor to do the work of sanctification in their hearts after salvation. The Watchtower Society interprets the Bible for their followers, so they do not need the Holy Spirit to "guide [them] into all truth" (John 16:13). They can live very comfortably without the Holy Spirit, because there is nothing supernatural about their religion.

CONCLUSION

After comparing biblical Christian teachings with those of the Watchtower Society, it should be evident to anyone who knows the Bible that their teachings are not based on the Bible. The Witnesses need to hear the true gospel that offers salvation through the precious blood of the Lord Jesus Christ. Christians should have a burning desire to share this truth with them, though it will take a lot of prayer and time. However, it is worth all that effort when someone comes out of the error of a man-made organization into the glorious freedom found in Christ.

The next chapter will examine the "fruits" that the Watchtower Society offers as evidence that they are the true religion and will show why these fruits are not valid.

CHAPTER SIX

BY THEIR FRUITS YE SHALL KNOW THEM

The Jehovah's Witnesses claim that they are the only approved organization of Jehovah God on earth. The following twelve claims were taken from a letter written by a Jehovah's Witness to a friend and are typical of Watchtower claims. After each claim I shall give an answer.

NEUTRALITY. *Jesus said, ". . . they are not of the world, even as I am not of the world" (John 17:14b, KJV). In essence, that means that Christians must be neutral toward politics.*

Jehovah's Witnesses will not vote, hold political office, work for government agencies, or recognize the national flag. This is a later teaching, because for many years they were not neutral. If this teaching is correct, they violated God's law during those early years.

No government worker in the Bible was ever told to leave his job. John the Baptist did not tell the soldiers to leave the army. Peter did not tell Cornelius, a centurian, to give up his position. Philip did not tell the Ethiopian treasurer to quit his job. In the Old Testament, Joseph, Daniel, and Nehemiah were officials in pagan governments, yet the Bible itself calls them men of great faith.

In Matthew 22:21 Jesus indicated that we do have a responsibility to government when He told the Pharisee, "Render therefore unto Caesar the things which are Caesar's; and unto God the things that are God's."

The Jehovah's Witnesses are looking forward to the time when they will live on the new earth. However, they don't want to help make the present earth a better place in which to live while they are waiting.

KILLING AND WARFARE. *Christ said that we are not to kill and that a Christian should love his enemies as himself. How can you love your enemy if you kill him? Most of the "Christian" faiths have gone to war—"Christian" brother against "Christian" brother. I am talking about Catholics, all of the main Protestant groups, Mormons, and others. Jehovah's Witnesses have not and will not go to war.*

Not all of the mainline Protestant groups have gone to war. Several centuries before the Jehovah's Witnesses came into existence, the Moravians and the Mennonites, not to mention the Quakers and some others, were against war.

The statement "Jehovah's Witnesses have not and will not go to war" is incorrect. The writer either did not know the history of the Society or he ignored it. For the first sixty years of the movement they allowed their members to join the army and go to war. They didn't change this policy until 1940. If the Bible is against war, why did it take them so many years to find this out?

It is interesting to read in context the Bible reference about love. They render Luke 6:27–31 in the New World Translation as follows

But I say to you who are listening, Continue to love your enemies, to do good to those hating you, to bless those cursing you, to pray for those who are insulting you. To him that strikes you on the one cheek, offer the other also; and for him that takes away your outer garment, do not withhold even the undergarment. Give to everyone asking you, and from the one taking your things away do not ask (them) back. Also, just as you want men to do to you, do the same way to them.

Jehovah's Witnesses don't practice this kind of love.

They treat those disfellowshipped from the Society as enemies. The Witnesses will not speak to them or have anything to do with them, nor will they show a drop of love to them.

The Witnesses go door to door, but if you try to visit *them*, they will tell you to leave. Once I made an appointment with a Witness to come to my house ten times. He agreed to do so. However, he came only once, so I went to his house. After a short time, even though he was the one asking the questions, I was told to "leave in five minutes" or he would call the police. I left immediately, but he still called the police.

Another time, the Jehovah's Witnesses were in my area and left an invitation to come to their Kingdom Hall. I did go. After attending three meetings, people started talking to me and asking me questions—which I answered. In the middle of the conversation, as I was answering questions asked by a Witness, the elders told me to leave. I replied that I would leave when I finished the conversation. The elders called the police and had me put out of the hall. When I asked what I had done wrong, they only said that I had been told to leave.

I have never experienced any of the love that the Jehovah's Witnesses say that they show to their enemies. I should receive a lot of love from them! I do not hate the Jehovah's Witnesses, but I do hate their false teachings. I love the people and want to win them to Christ.

UNPAID CLERGY. *Jesus specifically told his disciples not to charge for their services. Our beloved brother Paul never charged for his spiritual services and did secular work so that he would not be a "burden" to the brothers. There is no scriptural principle for setting up a special "clergy" class. In fact, ALL early Christians were ministers. Jehovah's Witnesses follow the above scriptural principles; few other so-called Christian groups do. We do ask for a contribution for the publications that we distribute door-to-door, but that only covers the cost of printing and publishing. No profit is made.*

A person who would make this statement does not know Church history or what the Bible teaches. Yes, true servants of God do not charge for their services, but the Bible does teach that those in the ministry should live by the ministry. First Corinthians 9:13–14 says, "Do ye not know that they which minister about holy things live of the things of the temple? and they which wait at the altar are partakers with the altar? Even so hath the Lord ordained that they which preach the gospel should live of the gospel." In the Old Testament, the Levites were to be supported by the people; and in the New Testament, Christ Himself chose some who were to go into full-time service for Him.

The Society says that Paul did secular work, but they don't mention that he only did it for a short time. They also ignore the fact that Paul received most of his income from offerings taken by the churches where he had ministered. The Society also ignores the fact that Jesus instructed at least five of His disciples to leave their secular jobs and to follow Him in full-time service.

Luke 8:1–3 says, "And it came to pass afterward, that he [Jesus] went throughout every city and village, preaching and shewing the glad tidings of the kingdom of God: and the twelve were with him, and certain women . . . and many others, which ministered unto him of their substance." This passage shows us that Jesus and the disciples received offerings from people.

The members of the governing body of the Watchtower Society do not work for their living but are supported by the organization. Also, they pay their district overseers. What is the difference between them and the clergy? They say that they don't pay these men very much, but they are paid! (They should be ashamed of themselves for not paying very much, because 1 Timothy 5:18 says, "The labourer is worthy of his reward.")

The Society uses the argument that they don't have paid clergy in order to "prove" that theirs is the only true religion. Most of the other cults, such as Mormonism and the Unification Church, also do not have paid clergy. Does this mean that all of these cults have the truth?

When a Witness says that the Society does not make a profit from the donations he receives from the literature he distributes when going door to door, he either does not know how the organization is operated or he is lying. Seventy percent of the income of the Watchtower Society comes from the profit they make from the donations they receive for their literature. Only thirty percent comes from the offerings of the people.

The Witnesses apparently do not give much money to their organization. One night, I was at a Kingdom Hall when they reported their offerings for the month. There were at least fifty adults in that congregation. Their total offerings for the month were less than I had personally given to the Lord's work that month.

AVOID PAGAN DOCTRINES AND PRACTICES. *A careful study of the Bible and other recognized authorities will show that many of today's "Christian" holidays are not Christian at all, but are PAGAN. An encyclopedia will give you the Babylonian origin of Christmas, Halloween, Mother's Day, birthdays, Easter, and New Year's Day. Jehovah's Witnesses do not celebrate such pagan holidays. Second Corinthians says, "Get out of the unclean thing." Have you? I have.*

The Jehovah's Witnesses will use what they call "recognized authorities" only if they think that these authorities agree with what the Society teaches.

For many years, the Watchtower Society celebrated these "pagan" holidays. Charles Russell observed Christmas and thanked people for their Christmas gifts. If it is so obvious that the Bible condemns these holidays, why didn't Charles Russell know this? Does this mean that he had not carefully studied the Bible?

It was not until sixty years after the Society began that

they started to condemn such practices. Why did it take so long for them to learn that these holidays are pagan?

The Watchtower Society is strong on stating that certain holidays are pagan because they are on the same day as pagan holidays were once celebrated. But to celebrate a holiday on the same day that a pagan holiday was once celebrated does not make it pagan. Most people are not aware that pagans celebrated on these days. Neither do most people celebrate these holidays for the same reason the pagans celebrated theirs. Besides, the Jehovah's Witnesses are inconsistent because they do not refuse to use the *calendar*, even though most of the days and months are named after pagan gods.

The writer confuses the issues because he includes Christian practices with those which are not. New Year's Day has never been a Christian holiday, as far as I know.

The only time Christmas is celebrated in the Bible is when God sent the angels to announce Christ's birth to the shepherds. I don't think God can be accused of being pagan. It has been taught that December 25 was set as the date to celebrate Christ's birth by the Emperor Constantine on what was a pagan holiday. However, Harold W. Hoehner in his book, *Chronological Aspects of the Life of Christ* (Zondervan, 1979), shows that Christmas was celebrated on December 25 almost back to the time of the New Testament church.

For the Christian, Christmas is a time to celebrate the birth of Christ who came to be our Savior. Because the unsaved person celebrates Christmas in a different way does not make the holiday pagan.

I don't know where the Jehovah's Witnesses find Mothers' Day in the Bible. A Christian started Mother's Day in 1908 to honor godly mothers. The Bible says, "Honor thy father and mother" (Eph. 6:2). It is not pagan to obey the Bible.

Easter is definitely not pagan. The practice of meeting for worship on Sunday instead of Saturday began very early as a way of remembering Christ's resurrection on the first day of the week. Even the Jehovah's Witnesses meet on Sunday. If it is acceptable to remember Christ's resurrection every Sunday, then having a special remembrance once a year can't be pagan.

The Watchtower Society only condemns certain practices, and they are not consistent. For example, they will not celebrate birthdays, but they do celebrate weddings with drinking and other "pagan" practices. They don't condemn drinking alcoholic beverages. Instead, they try to justify it from the Bible. They say that you should not drink in excess, but they refuse to admit that alcohol controls those who use it.

UNSCRIPTURAL DOCTRINES AND TEACHINGS. *The doctrines of the trinity, hellfire, immortality of the soul, that everyone dies and goes to heaven, Israel's covenant relationship with God, Mary as the mother of God, the Pope as infallible, the cult of the priesthood, etc., are sincere attempts to explain the Bible. Unfortunately, they are all unscriptural. I can use any Bible translation and easily disprove any or all of them. Any Jehovah's Witness can do the same. Jehovah's Witnesses do not teach any unscriptural pagan doctrines.*

Read 1 Corinthians 15. It tells us that at the end of the thousand years, Jesus returns the kingdom to his Father and is subject to the Father. No trinity here. Jesus and God are separate individuals with separate personalities who are united in will and purpose but are not equal. I have looked up hundreds of scriptures in all the standard translations that disprove the doctrine of the trinity.

The hellfire doctrine is unscriptural and perverted. The scriptural references to hellfire are symbolic for the absolute destruction of the wicked and do not mean eternal torment.

THE TRINITY

The Jehovah's Witnesses mix all of the beliefs of the so-called Christian groups and infer that they all believe the same thing. It is the same as if I declared that since both Mormonism and the Watchtower Society are cults, they believe the same things. Born-again Christians would condemn some of the practices that the writer mentioned, such as the infallibility of the Pope.

When Charles Russell began the Watchtower movement, he embraced the liberal teachings of that day. The liberals denied the deity of Jesus Christ and the Trinity. Now, the Jehovah's Witnesses condemn these groups, even though they share some of the same beliefs.

Approximately eighty percent of the quotes they use to disprove the Trinity are misquoted from the writings of Trinitarians. An article trying to disprove the Trinity appeared in the August 1, 1984, issue of *The Watchtower* (pp. 20–24). They take all six of the quotes out of context from articles that *prove* the Trinity. Three of these quotes came from the writings of J.N.D. Kelly, who is a sound Trinitarian. The Witnesses also often misquote Robert Dick Wilson, a Greek scholar and Trinitarian.

Fifteen percent of the quotes used to try to disprove the Trinity came from secular works such as the *Encyclopedia Britannica*. The articles in the *Encyclopedia Britannica* seek to prove (not disprove) the Trinity and the literal bodily resurrection of Christ. Only five percent of the quotes used by the Society come from Unitarians or others who deny the Trinity.

The Jehovah's Witnesses use the book *The Two Babylons* by Rev. Alexander Hislop to try to prove their point. However, once again they misquote what the author said. Rev. Hislop was a Christian who believed in the Trinity. The publishers of his book, Loizeaux Brothers, are known for their strong Trinitarian publications.

By denying the Trinity, the doctrine of hell and the immortality of the soul, the Watchtower Organization (and all the many other groups who deny these teachings) actually creates more problems than they solve. (It is best not to discuss these issues in your early discussions but wait until your callers have begun to do a little thinking.)

By remembering the following line of reasoning, you will be helped a great deal in your witnessing. Here is my approach:

We know that the doctrine of the Triune God is clearly based upon the Bible. However, let us look at the complex problem the Watchtower has created by not believing in this doctrine of the Trinity.

The Bible teaches that there is only one God. If you think through what the Watchtower Society teaches, in reality they have two distinct gods. They believe that the Father is the eternal God but that He created the Son, "a god" according to John 1:1 in their Bible, the New World Translation. This gives them two separate gods. To believe in two gods is polytheism, which is a pagan doctrine. (They accuse Christians of being pagan because they believe in the Trinity, but *they* are the ones who really are pagan.)

The Watchtower tries to justify this belief by saying that angels are sometimes called "sons of God" (Job 1:6; 2:1; 38:7), and also by using verses where the word "gods" is mentioned. John 10:34 is a quote from Psalm 82:6; when "gods" is read in context, however, these verses show clearly that "gods" refer to human judges who will die as all other men. In 1 Corinthians 8:5 the text again uses the word "gods." But when one reads the verse before it, which is part of the context, he learns that "there is none other God but one." How could it be taken that here the Bible teaches more than one God? It become obvious that the way they try to justify having two gods does not hold any weigh.

(Though very few Jehovah's Witnesses realize it, because it is sort of a hidden doctrine, the Watchtower Society teaches that each of the 144,000 in heaven will be just as much a god as Christ is. They do not believe that the 144,000 just *help* Christ reign during the Millennium. Rather, they have *equal power* with Him! So in reality, the Watchtower teaches that there are *many* "gods.")

John 17:3 reads, in the New World Translation, "This

means everlasting life, their taking in knowledge of you, the only true God, and of the one whom you sent forth, Jesus Christ." If there is *only one true God*, then the logical conclusion is that all other "gods" have to be "false gods." Since they proclaim that the Father is the true God, then the created "son-god" of the Watchtower must be a false god! (The Jehovah's Witness you are talking to should be pressed on these points. Since the Son to them is only "a god," then he has to be a "false god"—since there can be only one true God!)

But this is not the end of the problem. As I said before, they believe that the Son is a created being who lives only in heaven. But at the time he was created, he was merely "a god." However, in Isaiah 9:6 it speaks about the Son being "The mighty God." (They will be quick to say he is "The mighty God" but not the "Almighty"—like the Father.) And in order for them to have Him become "The mighty God," they propose that the Son—whom they claim willed himself out of existence at the time Jesus was born on this earth—was re-created three days after the death and annihilation of the man Jesus Christ. It was at *this* time, they argue, that the re-created Son became the "Mighty God" (NWT). But they do not believe that he will *continue* in that state. They say that after the 1000-year reign of Christ, the Son will turn over the kingdom to the Father, and they interpret this as meaning that the re-created Son will be demoted to "a god." I do not understand how "a god" could will himself out of existence and later become the "Mighty God" for at least 3000 years and then go back to being only "a god"! Thus, by denying the Trinity, many perplexing problems are created.

Here are a few other problems left unsolved by denying the Trinity:

Ask them to explain the condescension of Christ clearly from the Bible. As just mentioned, the Watchtower Society teaches that at the time Jesus was born on this earth the Son in heaven "willed himself out of existence" so that the "life-force" (spirit) of the Son could came down from heaven. In this way Jesus Christ could claim that there was a connection between himself and the Son. But what is the Watchtower explanation of a "life-force"? To them it is only the "breath" that keeps a human being alive. It lacks personality. It cannot think, speak, hear, see, or feel. Since there is absolutely nothing *in* the "life-force" (it is only breath), then really *nothing* came down from heaven. When clearly questioned about this, they simply do not have any convincing answers. But it can become even a little more involved. They say that the Son was a "spirit creature" who lived in "a spirit body" (whatever that might be). But since spirit bodies do not have blood in them, they do not need the oxygen from air—so they would not have any "breath" or "life-force." To me, this all sounds very mysterious and complicated.

Take the resurrection of Jesus Christ. The word *resurrect* means "to stand up again." In other words, the person who died will be raised to life. The Bible mentions the resurrection of Jesus Christ over one hundred times. The Watchtower Society teaches that Jesus gave his life as a "ransom," and says that if Jesus had been bodily resurrected from the dead he would have *taken back* the "ransom." (Don't ask me to explain this, because I have never found a J.W. who would attempt to do so.) They teach instead that Jesus was raised as "a spirit." Of course there is not one single verse in the Bible that would even give the slightest hint of such a teaching.

I questioned many Jehovah's Witnesses about this "a spirit" for eight years before I got any kind of explanation. As I wrote in "The Contrast Between Biblical Christianity and Watchtower Beliefs" (See Chapter 5, page 72), they take the word "spirit" from 1 Peter 3:18 and the word "a" from 1 Corinthians 15:44 and make up the expression "a spirit." You are just supposed to know that this "a spirit" is the re-created Son who willed himself out of existence when Jesus was born upon this earth.

Ask the Jehovah's Witness you are dealing with to show you very clearly from the Bible their explanation of the re-creation of the Son and where in the Bible it is taught that spirit beings have "spirit bodies." Also, since Jesus Christ was completely annihilated at the time of His death, how can they continue to talk about Jesus Christ being in heaven or being able to reign? How can something that is annihilated somehow reign?

Ask them upon what scriptural ground the Son, who was first created as "a god," becomes "the mighty God" after being re-created. I can't understand why the Father would give the re-created Son such an exalted position for just committing suicide!

The Watchtower Society has another major problem along this line. Since they deny the Trinity, they must have "two creators." Jesus is one creator and Jehovah is the other. In John 1:3 in the New World Translation, where it is speaking about Jesus, it clearly says: "All things came into existence through him, and apart from him not even one thing came into existence."

Again, creation is ascribed to Jesus in Colossians 1:16. It literally reads, according to the Watchtower publication *The Kingdom Interlinear Translation of the Greek Scriptures*, as: "because in him it was created the all (things) in the heavens and upon the earth, the (things) visible and the (things) invisible, whether thrones or lordships or governments or authorities the all (things) through him and into him it has been created."

However, the Bible emphatically declares that Jehovah *alone* created everything. Isaiah 44:24 reads: "This is what Jehovah has said, your Repurchaser and the Former of you from the belly: 'I, Jehovah, am doing *everything*, stretching out the heavens *by myself*, laying out the earth. Who was with me?'" (NWT) [italics added].

To the Jehovah's Witness, Jehovah and Jesus are two separate "gods." Thus Jesus created all things, and yet Jehovah created everything by Himself. Surely this is an impossibility! Yes, J.W.'s need to be shown that by denying the Trinity they have created more problems than they thought they solved.

When you mention to a Jehovah's Witness that the Trinity

teaching is somewhat a "mystery," they will laugh at such an idea. But when you begin to question them concerning the Holy Spirit, this *really* is a mystery. The Watchtower Society denies the personality of the Holy Spirit and speaks of "it" as "God's active force." If you ask them to explain what they mean, you are certain not to get a clear explanation. They might venture that it is something like a "radio wave," but that is about all the illlumination you will get. The Watchtower is great at attacking the beliefs of other groups, but give no real elucidation of what they believe. By requesting that they give you an understandable explanation of the nature of the Holy Spirit you are going to have them confounded—because they cannot give one.

The Bible says in Mark 3:29 that the sin of blasphemy against the Holy Spirit is the unpardonable sin. It is very strange that the greatest sin that can be committed is against the impersonal active force of God. How can you speak against something that does not exist except as energy?

The Holy Spirit speaks. I would like to have a Jehovah's Witness tell me how an impersonal "active force" can speak. How does the "active force" empower people? How can an "it" comfort? How can an "it" teach? How can an "it" encourage? These are real questions with which a Jehovah's Witness must be faced.

It is strange that angels are "spirit beings" but are real personalities and are alive. We know that angels can speak, guide, encourage, etc. The Bible speaks of the Holy Spirit doing much more than any angel, but He is denied personality by the Watchtower Society and is degraded to just an active force.

HELL AND PUNISHMENT

What happens when a person or an organization denies the doctrine of hell? The only conclusion you can come to is that *God is very unjust.* The Watchtower Society teaches that "the wages of sin is death," and understands this to mean that when you die you pay the wages for all your sins. But to them, there is no pain or punishment in death; it is just like going to sleep. If this is a fact, then the person who has murdered ten people, has been a drunkard, has beaten his wife and family and committed many other sins, will experience exactly the same end as the child who only took two cents from his mother's pocketbook. That is not justice. But that is what you have to believe if you deny there is any punishment after death. (Even Satan and all the wicked angels will be punished by being annihilated, the Watchtower teaches.) Not only will the god of the Watchtower neglect punishing anyone for his or her sins, but just about all people who have ever lived will be resurrected and live in a beautiful paradise here upon this earth . . . which the Jehovah's Witnesses will first have to build by manual labor.

Though the unjust Watchtower god will never punish sin—not even the very worst—yet he is very severe to the Jehovah's Witnesses. According to the teachings of the Watchtower Society, the most severe punishment that can be inflicted upon a person is to be irreversibly annihilated at the end of this life and never have an opportunity to enter paradise. But this is the fateful destination of nearly one third of those who join the organization—and are later disfellowshipped.

Note this: a J.W. must be in one hundred percent submission to *everything* the Society teaches and commands. If a J.W. father sends a birthday card to his non-Witness son, and is caught and does not repent of it, he will be disfellowshipped from the Watchtower organization. This means he will be irreversibly annihilated at the end of this life. If a J.W. wife hears an elder speak something from the platform that she doesn't agree with, and she as much as frowns—and he sees her—she will be disfellowshipped if she does not repent when confronted by the elders.

You can even be disfellowshipped for something that is not forbidden in the Bible. In 1967 the Watchtower Society forbade any kind of organ transplant. If a person was going blind and received a corneal transplant, they would disfellowship him. But in 1980 the organization revoked this rule and instead left it up to the individual to decide. However, they would not reverse themselves and reinstate any person who had a transplant, even though that person had not violated any biblical principle but only a rule that the human organization itself later changed.

These are just a few examples of the very small infractions that can cause a Jehovah's Witness to be disfellowshipped. While their god will not eternally punish any kind of evil among those who are *not* Jehovah's Witnesses, he is very, very severe to those who claim to have the only true religion. They can be damned forever!

This still does not satisfy the Watchtower Society, because it takes upon itself to see that all disfellowshipped Witnesses get punished *right now*. When a person becomes a Jehovah's Witness, he or she is strongly urged to break off friendship with all who are not J.W.'s. This includes even one's immediate family. But worse yet—when a J.W. gets disfellowshipped, no J.W. will have anything to do with that person. For example, if your children and grandchildren are still in the organization, they will speak to you only when there is necessary business. Even then they will not be civil to you. I don't know anything more awful that could happen to a person in this life than to have absolutely no friends and no close relationship with relatives—but this is the dire punishment inflicted upon the disfellowshipped Jehovah's Witnesses by their god who is supposed to be a "god of love."

This is a frightful teaching. Their god will never eternally punish any *wicked* people. In fact, he will give them a second chance on a beautiful earth. But a faithful Jehovah's Witness who is less than one hundred percent in submission to a human organization can be forever annihilated for one small infraction and never given an opportunity to go on to their new earth.

And that is not all! As I see it, the god of the Watchtower is not only merciless to those disfellowshipped; he is very severe to those who remain loyal. Let me explain. Jehovah's Witnesses teach that Armageddon will soon come. Then the earth will be almost completely destroyed. Their books show cities being leveled by earthquakes and fire. They imply that there will be a nuclear war which will cause great destruction. With such mass obliteration there will be no more roads, electric lines, mechanized equipment, etc. There will be over five billion bodies lying around. The wicked are destroyed; but as we mentioned, death is only falling asleep, so their being destroyed is to them not a problem. But the "lucky" Jehovah's Witnesses, who are the only ones to survive, will first have to dispose of the billions of bodies and then by manual labor work for scores of decades to build a perfect paradise upon this earth. Not one trace of the old society is to be left.

But why are these "lucky" Jehovah's Witnesses working so hard? It is so that God can resurrect all the wicked people who have ever lived (except disfellowshipped Jehovah's Witnesses) that they may enjoy the beautiful earth which the Jehovah's Witnesses have worked so hard to build. For at least the first five hundred years of the Millennium, the Jehovah's Witnesses must continue to build houses and make gardens for all those who will be raised, so that they may have a place in which to live.

To me it seems the J.W.'s have everything reversed! If the wicked survived and had to build a paradise for the Jehovah's Witnesses, I could understand their teaching. But for the "righteous" (?) to have to work so hard to build a beautiful place for the "wicked" to enjoy—well, it seems to me that God is actually punishing the Jehovah's Witnesses and showing His kindness to the wicked!

IMMORTALITY OF THE SOUL

The Watchtower Society's denial of the immortality of the soul leaves many questions which are impossible for them to answer. They teach that "the soul is not a part of man that separates from the body at death and goes on living. . . . Since the human soul is man himself, then it cannot be some shadowy thing that merely inhabits the body or that can exist apart from the person. . . . The human soul possesses physical qualities. . . . Souls have blood traveling through their veins. . . . Yes, your soul is really YOU, with all your physical and mental qualities."

As evidence that the soul is physical, a J.W. may point to Bible verses in which the word "soul" is used to mean the entire person. For instance, Genesis 2:7: "And the LORD God formed man of the dust of the ground, and breathed into his nostrils the breath of life; and man became a living soul." Or Jeremiah 2:34, which speaks of "the blood of the souls of the poor innocents." Or Ezekiel 18:4b: "The soul that sinneth, it shall die."

Is this a problem? It need not be. We readily admit that an entire person is often called a soul—"My, you're a restless soul," etc. Man very definitely *is* a soul; but he "is a soul" expressly because he does "have a soul."

The use of the word "soul" for the entire individual is simply a *synecdoche*, a common figure of speech in which the name of the most important part of a thing is applied to the entire object. Thus a woman may speak of purchasing "a pair of heels," meaning a pair of high-heeled shoes. A mariner may call out, "I see five sails," meaning not sails alone but five sailboats. A tourist may rave about the mighty peaks in Switzerland, but he has reference to the entire mountains, not just their peaks. Or we may speak of autumn as "fall," not because the falling of leaves occurs every day of the season or is its only activity, but because this is the *most important* event of the season. And referring to the entire individual as a soul, since it is truly his most important part, is simply another use of *synecdoche*—a figure of speech found in nearly all languages from earliest times.

While claiming that the soul is physical, the Society teaches that 144,000 "souls" will go to heaven—and these "souls" are *not* human bodies. So what really goes to heaven? They propose that these "souls" will be clothed in "heavenly bodies" (never described). But they teach that a physical body is necessary to be yourself. When pressed on this point, they have no reasonable answer.

This idea of denying the immortality of the soul has other serious implications. If a soul cannot exist without a body, then it is only logical that a soul ceases to exist when a person dies physically. Yet they teach that in the resurrection people will not receive the *same* body that they had here upon the earth, but a *new* body—which in some way will be similar to the body they had on earth, because they can be recognized. But if the real person has to have physical qualities, and they receive a different body than that which they had upon this earth, then they are not really the same person! They say that the personal traits of a person are kept in store in the mind of God while the body is annihilated; but if God later creates a different body and puts the personality of the person in that body, then it cannot be the same person that lived upon the earth! Therefore, it is impossible for them to teach that you, *yourself*, will ever live again in the future upon paradise earth.

Jehovah's Witnesses have never considered the results of their denial of the Trinity, hellfire, and the immortality of the soul. And so you can make much more progress with them by trying to get them to explain their teachings to *you* than by trying to explain your teachings to *them*. (This can be done later, when the heart is prepared.) It will be very hard for them to defend what they deny, and your queries will help in opening them up to the truth.

USE OF GOD'S NAME. *The Bible teaches that it is important to know and use God's name. It specifically gives us his name in Psalm 83:18 which says, "That men may know that thou, whose name alone is JEHOVAH, art the most high over all the earth."*

In John 17:26, Jesus says that he knows and uses the divine name of God. The Lord's Prayer in Matthew 6 commands us to sanctify God's name. Unfortunately, most Bible translations used by so-called Christian faiths do not contain the divine name. Paul stated in Romans 10:13 that "For everyone who calls on the NAME OF JEHOVAH will be saved." (NWT) *Paul is directly quoting the Hebrew Scriptures, and in the Hebrew, they use the name "Jehovah."*

The New World Translation of the Bible, used extensively by the Jehovah's Witnesses, uses "Jehovah" in all the thousands of places where it was used in the original Hebrew and Greek Scriptures. Does your church use God's name? Who is internationally known for using it? The Jehovah's Witnesses!

It is strange that Jehovah's Witnesses condemn other groups for not using the Hebrew word "Jehovah" when they do use the equivalent word, "Lord." J.W.'s need to be reminded that for fifty years *they* used other names for God besides Jehovah. It wasn't until 1931 that the Society began using "Jehovah" exclusively.

The name "Jehovah" by itself does not have any meaning for the average person. The Hebrew word "Jehovah" must be explained in a person's native tongue for him to understand it. The name "Jehovah" means "Lord." It also means "the self-existent one." It expresses His:

1. Love—Jeremiah 31:3
2. Righteousness or justice—Psalm 11:7
3. Holiness—Leviticus 19:2

Jehovah is the redemption name of Deity. Salvation by Jehovah without sacrifice is unknown in Scripture. The character of Jehovah is expressed in Judges 6: Jehovah hates and judges sin (vv. 1–5); Jehovah loves and saves sinners (vv. 7–18); and salvation comes only through sacrifice (vv. 19–21). The name of Jehovah cannot be understood without a correct knowledge of the Lord Jesus Christ, who was the sacrifice for our sins.

The Bible uses many different names for God. All of these should be referred to if we want to know what God is really like. An illustration of this is my family name "Lingle." The name by itself does not give much information about me. The average person would not know if I am German,

English, French, American, or another nationality. If I mentioned the name "Kawaguchi," the average American would not know if it were Japanese, Chinese, or Korean. (It's Japanese.) Even if they knew it is Japanese, they probably would not know that Kawaguchi means "the entrance or mouth of the river." Using only a person's family name tells you very little about the person.

If I were to add the name "Wilbur" to Lingle, you would know I am a male. If I told you that I am American, married, have five children, am six feet tall and weigh 170 pounds, you would know a little more about me. If I added that I am blond and light-skinned, you would know even more. However, you still would not know how much education I have, whether I am rich or poor, and if I am easy or difficult to get along with. You would not know if I am honest, trustworthy, sincere, or hard-working.

To really know a person, you need to know much more than just his or her family name. But a mountain of facts alone, however accurate, cannot tell you what a person is *truly* like. To learn that, you must get to know him *personally*.

Christians have no problem with using the name "Jehovah" for God; but they not only tell people *about* God, they tell people how they can know God *personally*.

To a Jehovah's Witness, the names "Jehovah" and "Father" designate the same person, though the expression "Lord Father" is never found in the Bible. Actually, the Father can be known only through the *Son*. Jesus declares, "All things are delivered unto me of my Father: and no man knoweth the Son, but the Father; neither knoweth any man the Father, save the Son, and he to whomsoever the Son will reveal him" (Matt. 11:27). And John 14:6 records that "Jesus saith unto [Thomas], I am the way, the truth, and the life; no man cometh unto the Father, but by me."

In order for a person to know the Father, he must come to Him through the saving blood of Jesus Christ. The Father rejoices when Christ is exalted because through Christ a sinner can come into the presence of the Father and worship

Him. The name "Jesus" is just as important as the name "Jehovah."

While Jehovah's Witnesses use the name "Jehovah," they seem to have no desire to know God in a personal way.

Any person interested in knowing God should study all the biblical names that explain who God is. There are very few Witnesses who can give you more than four names for God, and most do not know what the names mean.

Listed below are sixteen Hebrew words and phrases used for God, with their meaning and a Scripture reference:

1. *ADONAI*—Sovereign, master, owner of all things (Gen. 15:1–8).

2. *EL*—God, the powerful One (Isa. 40:12–18).

3. *ELOHIM*—The supreme One; signifies the one who completely possesses all the divine attributes and who makes covenants (Gen. 6:13–18).

4. *EL-GIBBOR*—Mighty God (Isa. 10:21).

5. *EL-SHADDAI*—Almighty God, symbol of changelessness and enduring strength (Gen. 17:1–8).

6. *EL-ELYON*—God Most High (Gen. 14:18–22).

7. *EL-OLAM*—The Eternal God (Gen. 21:33).

8. *EL-ROI*—The God who sees me, or The God who cares (Gen. 16:13).

9. *JEHOVAH*—The self-existent One (Ex. 3:14–15).

10. *JEHOVAH-SABAOTH*—Lord of hosts, or Lord of armies (1 Sam. 17:45).

11. *JEHOVAH-JIREH*—The Lord will provide (Gen. 22:14).

12. *JEHOVAH-NISSI*—The Lord is my banner (Ex. 17:15).

13. *JEHOVAH-RAPHA*—The Lord who heals (Ex. 15:26).

14. *JEHOVAH-SHALOM*—The Lord our peace, or The Lord sends peace (Jud. 6:23–24).

15. *JEHOVAH-TSIDKENU*—The Lord our righteousness (Jer. 23:6).

16. *JEHOVAH-SHAMMAH*—The Lord is present (Ezek. 48:35).

Once a person studies these names for God, he should realize the importance of using them so that God can be known in all His fullness.

UNITY OF FAITH. Paul stated in First Corinthians 1:10 that all Christ's followers should be completely united in the faith. Do we see this in the so-called mainline churches today? No! Many are arguing over doctrinal matters— conservatives versus progressives. Try to get a group of "Christians" together and see if they agree on the major teachings of the Bible. Just TRY. I challenge you!

If you gather a group of practicing Jehovah's Witnesses together (not disfellowshipped apostates), you can get agreement. All one in harmony; no dispolarity in the Kingdom.

Anyone can have a forced unity like that of the Watchtower Society. The members all read the same material and are forbidden to read any material that would cause them to question their beliefs. They are not allowed to talk to anyone who knows what is wrong with the Society's teachings. The members are forced to believe what they read so that they can claim unity. The Unification church, the Mormon church, and most other cults also claim such unity.

The writer says that there is unity among practicing Witnesses. But a person who does not attend meetings regularly would not be in unity with those who do. The teachings of the Society change so frequently that a non-attender would eventually believe things that the Society no longer taught, and thus there would be no unity.

The unity found among born-again Christians is not forced. It comes through the leading of the Holy Spirit, who guides each believer to the truth. Born-again Christians sometimes differ on minor issues, but they agree on the major doctrines of the Christian faith. If a Jehovah's Witness would compare the doctrinal statements of Bible-believing churches, he would see that they are basically the same.

For many years I was the chairman of a church for missionaries at a mountain resort in Japan. Everyone had to sign the same doctrinal statement to be a voting member of the church. People from at least thirty-five different groups signed that doctrinal statement.

On another occasion I was vice-chairman for an evangelistic meeting in our city. Most of the evangelical churches in the city (over eighty in number) cooperated. How does a Jehovah's Witness explain this if there is no unity among Christians? Why can I fellowship with missionaries from different groups or speak in many different churches if there is no unity?

CULTISM. *Your group accuses Jehovah's Witnesses of cultism. That's interesting considering the fact that we have more than four million active Witnesses WORLD-WIDE. We do not count individuals unless they are professed and active. The Anglican church claims millions of members, but less than ten percent are active (according to their own admission). We are the second largest religious group in Italy today. Hardly a cult.*

A cult professes to glorify an individual. Jehovah's Witnesses do not. We are not Russellites or Rutherfordites. We are Jehovah's Witnesses. NO SINGLE MAN IS GLORIFIED OR WORSHIPPED IN OUR ORGANIZATION.

We produce and print more religious literature than all of the so-called Christian churches combined. We can hardly be called a cult. Cults are concerned with their self-interests. We are concerned with Christ as king of that Kingdom.

The Witnesses argue that because they are both numerous and active, they have to be right. However, 2 Peter 2:1–2 tells us: "But there were false prophets also among the people, even as there shall be false teachers among you, who privily shall bring in damnable heresies, even denying the Lord that bought them, and bring upon themselves swift destruction. And *many* shall follow their pernicious ways; by reason of whom the way of truth shall be evil spoken of." This passage shows that numbers is not a test of right or wrong. If it were, the Mormons would come ahead of the

Jehovah's Witnesses, because they have a larger membership and are growing faster.

In spite of their denial, Jehovah's Witnesses were known for years as "Russellites." Russell was a man who was glorified and exalted for a while as th e "faithful and wise servant" of Matthew 24:45–47. However, they no longer consider him to be a great teacher because they realize that he was in error on many matters.

In the early 1970's, the Society abandoned the practice of having the leader run the whole show. They now operate under the direction of a governing body which has absolute rule. No one dares to question their teachings or their actions.

FALSE PROPHETS. *All of mankind is imperfect, including the Jehovah's Witnesses. Peter and Paul, the apostles, made serious mistakes, but continued making progress in Christian humility. Read Acts 1 and you will note that the early followers of Christ did not understand the timing of His return. No man on earth is perfect, nor is any religious organization. Without much difficulty, I can recite the major mistakes of some of the so-called churches of Christendom.*

The Watchtower Society is trying to cloud the issue to justify its false prophecies. The issue isn't whether God's servants are perfect or not, but whether they are true prophets when they claim to speak in the name of Jehovah.

The dates that the Society set for the Lord's return were presented as dates clearly taught in the Bible. The Watchtower followers were not given the freedom to reject what was taught because the Society claimed to be speaking in "the name of the Lord."

Deuteronomy 18:20–22 says:

But the prophet, which shall presume to speak a word in my name, which I have not commanded him to speak, or that shall speak in the name of other gods, even that prophet shall die. And if thou say in thine heart, How shall we know the word which the LORD hath not spoken? When a prophet speaketh in the name of the LORD, if the thing follow not, nor come to pass, that is the thing which the LORD hath not spoken, but the prophet hath spoken it presumptuously; thou shall not be afraid of him.

Since the Watchtower Society has made false prophecies, it is not worthy of the support of people who truly want to please Jehovah God. It needs to be exposed as an organization that has deceived its followers.

THE KINGDOM. *Jesus stated that his main object was to preach the good news of the Kingdom of God. Who is known internationally for this work? Not the churches of Christendom, but the Jehovah's Witnesses who are fulfilling Bible prophecy (Matthew 24:14). The future of mankind is only in God's real government, the Kingdom, with Jesus as King. Christendom is concerned with the Kingdom as "something within you." Hardly scriptural.*

Anyone who makes such a statement is not familiar with the Bible, because it states that we *are* to be concerned with what is within the heart. A person will never enter the kingdom of God if the right things are *not* in his heart.

First Corinthians 6:9–11 teaches:

Do you not know that the unrighteous shall not inherit the kingdom of God? Be not deceived: neither fornicators, nor idolaters, nor adulterers, nor effeminate, nor abusers of themselves with mankind, nor thieves, nor covetous, nor drunkards, nor revilers, nor extortioners, shall inherit the kingdom of God. And such were some of you: but ye are washed, but ye are sanctified, but ye are justified in the name of the Lord

Jesus, and by the Spirit of our God.

Those cleansed by the blood of Jesus will be the ones to inherit the kingdom of God.

The kingdom of God is not a matter of beautiful living conditions as the Society teaches. Romans 14:17 declares, "For the kingdom of God is not meat and drink; but righteousness, and peace, and joy in the Holy Ghost."

John 3:3 says, "Jesus answered and said unto him, Verily, verily, I say unto thee, Except a man be born again, he cannot see the kingdom of God." The gospel that we need to know is presented by Paul in 1 Corinthians 15:1–4. Verses 3 and 4 say, "For I delivered unto you first of all that which I also received, how that Christ died for our sins according to the scriptures; and that he was buried, and that he rose again the third day according to the scriptures."

The Bible never speaks about the "kingdom of this earth." It always speaks of the "kingdom of heaven" or the "kingdom of God." The Bible-believing Christians who teach that a person must be born again are the ones who are preaching the good news (or gospel) of the kingdom.

Up until 1935 the Watchtower Society did not teach that the kingdom of God was earthly. They said that their members would go to heaven to reign with Christ, and considered "heaven" and the "kingdom of God" to be the same place. However, once the membership approached 144,000, making the "heavenly class" nearly complete, they reversed their teaching and began equating the kingdom of God with the new earth.

Most Witnesses have no desire to be born again; therefore, they cannot enter the kingdom of God. The Society talks about the kingdom of God, but it does not preach the gospel of the new birth, and thus it is not preparing its members to enter the kingdom of God.

DOING GOD'S WILL. *Jesus noted in Matthew 7 that many would call upon him (so-called Christians), but*

that he would disown them because they are not doing the
will of his Father. Are you doing God's will? Do you teach
individuals about the kingdom of God, telling them that it is
a real government and the only hope for all of us, or are you
teaching personal salvation and belief in Christ as the only
important thing? Much more is involved.

Matthew 7:15–23 says that we are to test those who
claim to be prophets, warning us against those who are false
prophets. Therefore it condemns the practices of the Watchtower Society, because the things that they have "spoken in
the name of the LORD" have not come to pass. The Witnesses
will be the ones who are disowned.

What is the will of God? It is to recognize that I am a
sinner before God, to believe that Jesus Christ died on the
cross for all my sins (not just those inherited from Adam),
and to ask Him to be my Savior. Then, as a born-again
Christian, I will desire to live a life of holiness through the
power of the Holy Spirit. First Thessalonians 4:3 says, "For
this is the will of God, even your sanctification."

The Witnesses do not believe that a personal faith in
Jesus Christ as their Savior is necessary for entrance into the
kingdom. However, Christianity would have no meaning
without faith in Christ as a personal Savior. Jesus said, "I am
the way, the truth, and the life: no man cometh unto the
Father, but by me" (John 14:6). Only as Jesus Christ becomes
the center of a person's life can he really know and do the
will of God. Without personal salvation through Jesus Christ,
no one (including the Jehovah's Witnesses) will ever see the
kingdom of God.

THE BOTTOM LINE. *I personally feel and can scrip-*
turally support the statement that Jehovah's Witnesses are
the closest thing on earth today to the true Christian faith.
No one has ever given me a better alternative. If you can show
me a worldwide organization that meets the Bible's require-
ments for pure Christianity, then I will look elsewhere.

There is a worldwide organization that has far more to offer than the Watchtower Society. It is the Church of Jesus Christ, embracing all who have been born again. The Witnesses still carry the heavy burden of their personal sins. The Christian has been relieved of that burden by Christ's death for his sins. The Christian has been brought into God's family where he can have a personal relationship with Jehovah God—something that Jehovah's Witnesses lack. The Witnesses do not have the Holy Spirit to guide them into all truth.

The Watchtower Society is a human organization which keeps its members in bondage and attempts to run their entire lives. The born-again Christian has been brought into the freedom of Jesus Christ. Galatians 5:1 says, "Stand fast therefore in the liberty wherewith Christ hath made us free, and be not entangled again with the yoke of bondage."

No human organization will ever satisfy the longings of the human heart. Those longings can only be satisfied by faith in Jesus Christ. Satisfaction is found *in Christ*. Psalm 34:8 says, "O taste and see that the LORD is good: blessed is the man that trusteth in him."

The next chapter is the heart of this book because it presents the questions one should ask to get a Jehovah's Witness to question the Watchtower organization—an important step in leading him to Christ.

CHAPTER SEVEN

QUESTIONS TO ASK JEHOVAH'S WITNESSES

Witnessing to a Jehovah's Witness takes time because you must first teach him to think for himself. The Witnesses are taught to accept everything that the organization says without asking any questions. They are told that questioning the organization is the same as questioning Jehovah God. *It just isn't done!*

Your first task in witnessing to a Witness will be to get him to question what he has been taught so that he will begin to doubt the truthfulness of the organization. Until you do that, the Witness will not be interested in hearing anything you have to say.

The usual approach employed by a Christian witnessing to a Jehovah's Witness is to start questioning him about the Trinity, the deity of Christ, the immortality of the soul, hell, etc. This is something the Jehovah's Witnesses are expecting, so they have memorized an answer for each of your arguments. They hardly have to think in order to answer you, and if you happen to ask a question for which they don't know the answer, they can go and ask an elder or look up the answer in a Watchtower publication. Hence they still have not thought through the answer they have given you.

But when it comes to questions about the *organization*, that is different! Witnesses learn very early that they do not question the organization. If they dare to do so, they will be reprimanded severely—and they will know never to do that again! Take note: when you ask questions concerning their organization there is no individual or publication to which they can go for an answer. The Witness will have to begin to wrestle with the problem himself—and this is exactly what you want them to do.

The Watchtower Society realizes it is dangerous to let their followers know the true history of the organization, so has tried to develop ways to keep this knowledge from them. Even in their own publications, they not only twist the truth about other religious groups but they also falsify their own history. Therefore, questions about the organization are the best way to get Witnesses to think for themselves.

It is very difficult to convince people that they are wrong by just telling them so. You must let them reach that conclusion on their own, by giving them solid information to think about. Your goal should be to meet with the visiting Witness on a regular basis. It is best to limit each meeting to an hour. Take your time. Give him time to think about what you have discussed. If you push him into a corner immediately, he will not return, and you will have lost your opportunity to lead him to Christ.

The questions in this chapter are designed to get Jehovah's Witnesses to think about their organization. These are mainly thought-provoking questions, so you do not have to try to get them to give you a "right" answer. Actually, the seeds of doubt you sow through the questions are much more important than the answers they may give. Even though I have listed a possible answer to most of the questions, you are not likely to get the same answer from all Jehovah's Witnesses. Remember, these are brand-new questions which they have never heard before.

Since J.W.'s are not used to being logical or thinking for themselves, you may get some strange answers. But that is okay. You are getting them to think. There is no need to argue. When you receive a very strange answer you ought to repeat what the Witness has just said and then ask him if that is what he really meant to say. Sometimes, by your repeating his answer, he himself will realize that it wasn't a very convincing one. You can also bring it up again the next time you meet together, after he has had some time to think. You might say, "I have been thinking of what you said last week.

(Then repeat it.) I still don't understand how that answers my question. Do you have any further comments?"

You do not have to use these questions in any particular order. Use the ones with which you feel most comfortable. Nor do you have to use all of them. Once you have gotten the Witness to realize that the Watchtower Society is not reliable, then you can proceed to the next step: presenting the way of salvation.

Also, since the J.W. does not know where these questions are heading, he will often give an answer which, when you ask another question, he must then contradict. Here you can say, "I am a little puzzled! A while back you said such and such, and now you are saying something which seems to be different. To me this is a contradiction. Would you please explain this to me?" (Do not *tell* your visitors the answer, but *ask* them, so that they have to think and try to work it out for themselves.)

Nor are all the questions of the same importance. Some are merely what I call "tension breakers." To get the desired results, it is best not to ask the important questions all in a row. You should weave unimportant questions in with the important ones, so they will not become aware of your goal. And should there get to be a little tension, then back off and use a question that is really not important.

There are two possible reasons why a Witness might give an answer opposite to what I have given: (1) The Witness really does not know the correct answer, because the Watchtower Society has deliberately obscured the true history of the organization. (2) The Witness is lying to you, because there are some facts that he does not want you to learn too early in the conversation.

There are two major thrusts to these questions. Your first aim is to get the Witness to realize and admit that the Watchtower Society has no valid authority. Your second aim is to cause him to see that there have been many changes, false prophecies, contradictions, and much zigzagging back and forth—so their teachings can't be built upon eternal truths from God (which *never* can change!) but merely upon the dictates and changing ideas of the fallible men in their governing body. Witnesses keep talking about their "new light" that supposedly is getting rid of all pagan and apostate teachings. Since they claim they are *still* getting new light, this means that they still have pagan and apostate teachings left in the organization and do not yet have the pure truth. Thus, if one accepts the Watchtower teachings, then—by their own admission—one has to accept teachings that are wrong and which God hates.

Once you become familiar with the type of question which makes them think about the deep problems of the Watchtower organization, you will come up with your own. By all means, use them along with the questions in this book.

You will notice that I have often approached the same subject from two or three different angles. There are two reasons for this. First, a Jehovah's Witness might not grasp what you are driving at from the first approach, so you need to be able to question him on the same subject from a different angle. This should aid in the effectiveness of your witnessing. The second reason is that we have differing personalities, and some might feel better using one approach while another person would be much more comfortable using another approach.

Teaching a Jehovah's Witness to *think for himself* is well worth the effort. Yes, you may need to ask a question many times before he truly understands what you are asking and gives you a proper answer. But be persistent. As he begins to think for himself, it will get easier.

THE TRAINING OF FUTURE LEADERS

Question: The Society believes that the world will end very soon. They teach that the millennial kingdom (the 1000-year reign of Christ) will be governed by the Watchtower Society. If this is correct, why is the Society not training leaders for this job? Since you are not involved in current politics, where will your members get their training in how to run a government?

Response: Some of our present leaders might remain on the earth to reign during the Millennium.

Rebuttal: The Society teaches that all the present rulers are part of the 144,000, who will be in heaven during the Millennium. They do not accept the possibility that some of the 144,000 will remain on earth.

DETERMINING WHO IS RIGHT

Question #1: Many different groups (Watchtower Society, Mormons, Roman Catholics, Unification Church, etc.) claim that they are the only organization that represents Jehovah God on earth. Obviously, not everyone can be right. Each organization claims that it is right and all other organizations are wrong. A group that claims to be God's exclusive channel of communication to this earth should have distinctive doctrines which no other group has. Upon what distinctive doctrines does the Watchtower Society base *its* claim that it is the only true religious group?

Response #1: We do not believe in the pagan doctrine of the Trinity like other "Christian" groups do.

Rebuttal #1: That is interesting, because the Mormons, Moonies, The Way International, and many other groups also do not believe in the Trinity. If not believing in the Trinity makes the Watchtower Society the true religion, does it also make these other religions true? If many groups deny the Trinity, then this can't be claimed as a distinctive doctrine of the Watchtower Society. (The Jehovah's Witnesses have many arguments that they think disprove the Trinity. These arguments are found in the thirty-two page Watchtower Society booklet *Should You Believe in the Trinity?* (1984), as well as in their other literature. They concentrate their attack on other religious groups in the area of the Trinity and are well prepared to discuss this subject. Rebuttal #1 will block their arguments.)

Question #2: Since the denial of the Trinity is not a distinctive doctrine of the Watchtower Society, can you give me a doctrine that is distinctive?

Response #2: All the wars of Western history have been Christian wars where Christians fought against Christians. How can you say that you love your brother when you go to war and kill him? We are the only group that is against war.

Rebuttal #2: The Mennonites do not go to war, nor have they ever gone to war since they began several hundred years ago. The same is true of the Moravians. There are also the Quakers and the Seventh-Day Adventists who don't go to war. Do you acknowledge these groups as having the true religion since they don't go to war? Can't you give me some belief held only by the Watchtower Society?

Response #3: We are the only group that is against blood transfusions.

Rebuttal #3: The Watchtower Society is not the only group that is against blood transfusions. The Christian Scientists also do not believe in blood transfusions, so this is not a distinctive belief of the Watchtower Society.

Furthermore, the Society has been against blood transfusions only since 1945. (Most Witnesses will not know the exact year, but they usually know that it was sometime in the 1940's.)

The Witnesses teach that Jehovah God chose the Society to represent Him on earth in 1919 even though Charles Russell began teaching in 1880. Using the 1919 date means that for 26 years (1919 to 1945) members were allowed to get blood transfusions. Why did it take twenty-six years of "deep Bible study" to discover that blood transfusions are wrong? Why didn't God give "new light" on this at the beginning? Since the Society did not oppose blood transfusions for twenty-six years, this cannot be a distinctive doctrine that proves the validity of the Watchtower Society.

If you insist that this is a major doctrine, then the Society's claim that it was chosen by God in 1919 is false. The

Society did not begin doing God's will until 1945. Don't you have any distinctive doctrines or teachings?

Response #4: The Jehovah's Witnesses are known for preaching the "kingdom."

Rebuttal #4: The Mormons believe very strongly in the kingdom. They believe that they will be both the political and the religious rulers during the Millennium. They have already made plans how they will rule, unlike the Watchtower Society which has no plans at all. The leaders of your Society must all be members of the 144,000, which they claim go to heaven, so none of them will be left upon the earth.

Since Jehovah's Witnesses do not take part in government *now*, no one in the Society has the experience needed to run a civil government. It appears that Mormons believe more strongly in the kingdom than the Watchtower Society does.

Born-again Christians believe in the kingdom also. John 3:3 says, "Verily, verily, I say unto thee, Except a man be born again, he cannot see the kingdom of God." The Bible is clear on this point. To enter the kingdom, a person must experience a new birth through a personal relationship with Jesus Christ. The new birth should be taught by any group that believes in the kingdom.

Bible-believing churches teach about the new birth and the kingdom, so the Society is not the only group to teach about the kingdom. Clearly, the preaching of the kingdom is not a Watchtower Society distinctive. Doesn't the Society have any distinctive beliefs?

Response #5: God is a God of order. God has had an organization from the time of Adam and Eve until today. Since the Watchtower Society is an organization, it proves that it is doing God's will.

Rebuttal #5: Many other religious groups such as the Mormons, Roman Catholics, and the Unification Church are also known for their organizations. You still have not presented one doctrine that is distinctive. Can't you come up with even one?

Response #6: People recognize us as Jehovah's Witnesses when we go from house to house. We are known for using the name "Jehovah." We are the only group that uses Jehovah exclusively.

Rebuttal #6: I do not mind using the proper name for God, which is "Yahweh," but I don't like to use a false name for Him. If you will look up the name Jehovah in just about any dictionary or encyclopedia you will find that Jehovah is a false reading of the Hebrew word "Yahweh."

So far you have not given me even one distinctive teaching. Don't you have any?

BACKGROUND INFORMATION FOR THIS REBUTTAL

1. Some quotes from reference books on the name "Jehovah":

Webster's Third New International Dictionary: "Intended as a transliteration of Hebrew YAHWEH, the vowel points of Hebrew ADHONAY (my lord) being erroneously substituted for those of YAHWEH; from the fact that in some Hebrew manuscripts the vowel points of ADHONAY (used as a euphemism for YAHWEH) were written under the consonants YHWH of YAHWEH to indicate that ADHONAY was to be substituted in oral reading for YAHWEH. Jehovah is a Christian transliteration of the tetragrammaton long assumed by many Christians to be the authentic reproduction of the Hebrew sacred name for God, but now recognized to be a late hybrid form never used by the Jews."

Encyclopedia Americana: "JEHOVAH—an erroneous form of the name of the God of Israel."

Encyclopedia Britannica: "JEHOVAH—an erroneous rendering of the name of the God of Israel. The error arose among Christians in the middle ages through combining the consonants YHWH (JHVH) with the vowels of ADONAI. . . ."

New Catholic Encyclopedia: "JEHOVAH, false form

of the divine name Yahweh."

The Jewish Encyclopedia: "JEHOVAH is a mispronunciation of the Hebrew YHWH, the name of God. This pronunciation is grammatically impossible. The form 'Jehovah' is a philological impossibility."

Encyclopaedia Judaica: "YHWH. The personal name of the God of Israel is written in the Hebrew Bible with the four consonants YHWH and is referred to as the 'Tetragrammaton.' At least until the destruction of the First Temple in 586 B.C.E. this name was regularly pronounced with its proper vowels, as is clear from the Lachish Letters, written shortly before that date. . . . When Christian scholars of Europe first began to study Hebrew, they did not understand what this really meant, and they introduced the hybrid name 'Jehovah.'. . .

"The true pronunciation of the name YHWH was never lost. Several early Greek writers of the Christian Church testify that the name was pronounced 'Yahweh.' This is confirmed, at least for the vowel of the first syllable of the name, by the shorter form Yah, which is sometimes used in poetry."

(Note: One example is found in Psalm 68:4, which reads in the KJV: "Sing unto God, sing praises to his name: extol him that rideth upon the heavens by his name JAH, and rejoice before him." Even the Watchtower Society's NWT reads the same way. "Sing YOU to God, make melody to his name; raise up [a song] to the One riding through the desert plains as Jah, which is his name; and jubilate before him." This is a very strong argument to show that at least the first half of God's name was *not* lost as the Jehovah's Witnesses claim.)

2. Watchtower beliefs and explanations for the use of the name "Jehovah":

a. The Watchtower Society states that "Jehovah" was first used by the Spanish monk Raymundus Martini, in his book *Pugeo Fidei*, in 1270 A.D.

b. Joseph Rutherford claims that the name "Jehovah" was revealed to him in 1931 as the true name for God. From that time on, Watchtower followers have been known as Jehovah's Witnesses.

c. The Hebrew word translated LORD or Jehovah consists of four letters, all consonants. (Vowels were not written.) Known as "the tetragrammaton," these four letters are YHWH or JHVH when transliterated into English. The Hebrew people held this proper name in such high esteem that they would not pronounce it, and when reading the name aloud they spoke another name for God whenever it appeared. Scholars agree that "Yahweh" is its most accurate pronunciation.

d. The Watchtower Society acknowledges the fact that "Yahweh" is probably the proper pronunciation for God's name its 1984 booklet titled, *The DIVINE NAME That Will Endure Forever* (pp. 8–9).

The Watchtower Society claims they are responsible for putting God's name back in its proper place in the Bible and into general usage. However, when asked for an explanation as to why they continue to use Jehovah instead of the correct name "Yahweh," they contradict themselves by saying that the name Jehovah has come down through the ages as a well-known name for God—so most people are familiar with it. They say that people know who they are talking about when they use the word "Jehovah" but people are not familiar with the word "Yahweh."

The Watchtower claims that YHWH is written in the original New Testament as well as the Old Testament. In the New Testament of the Watchtower's New World Translation they have inserted the name Jehovah in 237 places—mostly where the Old Testament is quoted, but *not only* there. There are an estimated 5000 existing copies of Greek manuscripts of the New Testament. Though we do not have the original manuscripts, some go back very close to the originals and among these there is not one single manuscript found with YHWH written for the name "Lord."

But let us suppose the Watchtower Society is correct

(they are not) in putting the name "Jehovah" in the New Testament 237 times. They still have to face the fact that the original writings of the New Testament use the name "Jesus" 912 times. It seems obvious that the Holy Spirit wanted to give Jesus the preeminence in the New Testament.

It also should be noted that Jesus never addressed God as YHWH but always as Father, and this He did 260 times. When Jesus taught His disciples to pray, He said, "Our Father which art in heaven." The Jehovah's Witnesses continually address God as Jehovah God. They are not following the example of Jesus.

The Society says that when they make mistakes, they admit them and correct them. If this is true, they should now call themselves Yahweh's Witnesses. Why has the Society not made this change?

(What about *my* use of the name "Jehovah"? I am not against using the word "Jehovah" even though it is not the correct pronunciation. My point is to show the fallacy of the Watchtower's argument. If it is really so important to use the Hebrew word for LORD instead of the English word, and if they are so "accurate" and God *did* reveal this name to them, then they should at least use the word "Yahweh.")

Response #7: We use only the Bible to prove everything that we believe.

Rebuttal #7: I don't see how this can be a distinctive, because all so-called Christian groups make the same claim. Do you want to try again to give me a distinctive teaching?

Response #8: We have a unity which no other group has. All Witnesses worldwide believe the same thing. They all study the same thing simultaneously. Can you show me another group that has such unity?

Rebuttal #8: The Mormons, Unification Church, and others make the same claim. There are many church groups which study a predetermined subject each week.

(In the Japanese school system, each student in a particular grade studies the same thing at the same time as every other student in that grade. Does this unity make their school system the best in the world?)

Any group can have unity when they read only certain "approved" literature, are not allowed to read anything to the contrary, and must teach the same thing at the same time as others in the group. The only thing such unity shows is the degree of control the organization has over its members. It does not prove the truthfulness of their religion.

Doesn't the Society have any distinctives?

Response #9: We have a love existing among our members not found in any other group.

Rebuttal #9: In order for the Watchtower leaders to make such a claim, they would first have to attend meetings at many other churches so that they might speak from firsthand experience. However, since all the men on the governing body of the Watchtower Society had to be members of the Society before 1935 and since Jehovah's Witnesses are not allowed to attend any other religious meetings, the leaders have not had any firsthand experience for over sixty years. This makes it impossible for them to make a personal judgment on this matter of love. It is obvious that they are making a statement which they cannot prove.

I have attended many, many churches and at least seven different Kingdom Halls, so I think I have some basis on which to judge. I have never found any of this J.W. love that they are talking about. If you should dare to ask any thought-provoking questions, you will be ushered out of the Kingdom Hall in a hurry. If you don't move off right away, they will threaten to call the police. If you then do not leave, they will *actually* call the police. Just for asking one serious question!

(By this time, the Witness should realize that the Society lacks distinctive doctrines. He should realize that the Society has no valid basis for its claim that it is "God's sole channel of communication to this earth." You can go on to other questions at this point.)

ILLUMINATING THE BIBLE

Question #1: The Watchtower Society teaches that the Bible is inspired but must be properly explained ("illuminated") in order to be understood. The governing body of the organization is the only group supposedly qualified to do the illuminating. However, their illumination has changed many times. Why didn't God have the Bible illuminated when it was originally written? Wouldn't the authors of the books have been the best ones to do the job? Why did God make people wait 1,900 years to understand the Bible?

Response #1: (You probably will not get one.)

Question #2: Why did God write the whole Bible only for the 144,000? Why doesn't the whole Bible apply to everyone? It does not seem fair that God would exclude most people from being benefited by the teachings of the Bible!

Response #2: (You probably will not get one.)

CLAIMING OTHER GROUPS ARE WRONG

Question: There are religious groups in Christendom whose beliefs are the same as many of the Watchtower Society's beliefs. We call them liberals. They deny the Trinity, the deity of Christ, the bodily resurrection of Christ, the immortality of the soul, the teaching of hell, and they teach that most people will live in a paradise here on earth. Yet you do not differentiate between the groups which believe as you do and those that don't. You say that *all* of them are wrong. Why do you find fault with those who hold similar doctrines to yours? Please explain this way of thinking.

Response: (They do not know what other groups believe, so they will usually try to deny what you have said.)

PRAYING THE LORD'S PRAYER

Question: In many churches the congregations follow the example of Jesus in Matthew 6:9–13 and pray together the Lord's Prayer. They want to see the Father's name sanctified and His kingdom spread over all the earth. Do the Jehovah's Witnesses obey this command of Jesus and pray the Lord's Prayer weekly at any of their meetings? **Response:** No. (They might give various reasons for not doing so.)

READING OTHER BOOKS

Question #1: When one looks at the Watchtower publications he soon notices that the writers quote from many different books and encyclopedias in order to try to prove their beliefs and teachings. I would assume that the authors of the articles read these books in detail so as to be certain that they are quoting in context. Since they read and quote from so many sources, it seems to suggest that there are many good books on the market which are not written by Jehovah's Witnesses and yet contain a lot of truth that agrees with the Watchtower's teachings. Are you as a Jehovah's Witness free to read these various books?

Response #1: (If they are truthful they must say "No.")

Question #2: Why can the authors of the Watchtower publications in Brooklyn read these books but not the average Jehovah's Witness?

Response #2: (You probably won't get one, but this should make them think.)

PROVING THERE WAS AN EARLY ORGANIZATION

Question: Where did the organization ("mother") move to after the fall of Jerusalem in 70 A.D.? You teach that the organization in the book of Acts was the true church. You use Acts 15 to say that the organization is supposed to give commands to the church. What happened to this organization after the fall of Jerusalem?

Response: I do not know. I must research this.

Rebuttal: (If the above is their answer, ask the question again when you see them the next time. You can point out that early church history was recorded in great detail and is still with us today. There is no record that there was ever a central organization such as the Witnesses claim.)

EXPLAINING THE 144,000

BACKGROUND: The Watchtower Society teaches that the true church existed at the time that the book of Acts was formulated and that the Jerusalem church had the same kind of organization as the present Watchtower organization: therefore the apostolic church had to be the true church. Charles Russell believed and taught that the "anointed ones" began to be chosen just as soon as the church began, and by the end of the first century most of them were chosen. *The Watchtower* of February 1, 1975, reiterated that Jehovah God started selecting the 144,000 nineteen hundred years ago.

History tells us that this persecuted church continued for several centuries, so there were many years during which the true church existed and expanded. The Watchtower Society teaches that the 144,000 are the "worthy ones" chosen by God. Then surely the Christians in the early church would be among the 144,000!

The book of Acts mentions many thousands who were saved during the initial thirty years:

- 3,000 (Acts 2:41)
- daily saved (Acts 2:47)
- 5,000 (Acts 4:4)
- many (Acts 9:42; 17:12; 19:18)
- As many as were ordained to eternal life believed (Acts 13:48)
- many thousands [lit. *myriads:* tens of thousands] (Acts 21:20)
- many saints (Acts 26:10)

Adding these together would make a minimum of sixty to seventy thousand. Since the early Christians were persecuted, surely that would make them worthy to be among the

144,000—because they stood true to the faith.

Many local churches are mentioned in the New Testament. We know that these were once thriving churches which included many thousands of people. The Bible mentions churches in:

- Rome (Rom. 1:7)
- Corinth (1 Cor. 1:2)
- Galatia (Gal. 1:1)
- Philippi (Phil. 1:1)
- Ephesus (Eph. 1:1)
- Colosse (Col. 1:1)
- Thessalonica (1 Thess. 1:1)
- Crete (Tit. 1:5)
- Pontus, Cappadocia, Asia, and Bithynia (1 Pet. 1:1)
- Smyrna (Rev. 2:8)
- Pergamos (Rev. 2:12)
- Thyatira (Rev. 2:18)
- Sardis (Rev. 3:1)
- Philadelphia (Rev. 3:7)
- Laodicea (Rev. 3:14)

Even the Watchtower publication *REVELATION—Its Grand Climax at Hand!* acknowledges, on page 62, that Christianity was widespread. They quote McClintock and Strong's *Cyclopedia* (Vol. X, p. 519) which reports: "The administration of the younger Pliny as governor of Bithynia . . . was complicated with matters growing out of the rapid expansion of Christianity and the consequent rage of the heathen population within his province."

From the Bible and accurate church history we know that there were hundreds of thousands of true believers in the early years of the church. It has been estimated that there were at least 250,000 Jewish Christians alone, and that number may have been as high as one million.

One must be impressed by the many hundreds of thousands of martyrs who gave their lives for the faith, especially in the early church. A very conservative estimate would put the early church martyrs at 250,000. Some have mentioned the number as 800,000. (And the martyrs would only be a small fraction of the true and faithful believers of their day.) It is clear from the Bible that all martyrs go to heaven. Revelation 2:10 mentions the "crown of life" which is given to those who are "faithful unto death." From 2 Timothy 4:8 and other passages we deduce that crowns are given to those who go to heaven. And Revelation 6:9–11 makes it clear that those who are "slain for the word of God" will be in heaven.

Question #1: If the teaching is true that only 144,000 persons will go to heaven, I would like to know how there could possibly be any openings left when Charles Russell came upon the scene in 1880? The book of Acts mentions at least 60,000 people saved, and this was only the beginning of the growth of Christianity. Estimates have it that there were at least 250,000 Jews in the early church, not counting the thousands of Gentiles. Also there were over 250,000 martyrs who would surely be included in the 144,000. (In the Watchtower book *The Finished Mystery*, 1917, Charles Russell said there were 861,000 martyrs.) It seems obvious that these openings would all have been filled in the apostolic age or shortly thereafter.

Response #1: You have to realize that the Bible speaks about a falling away, so because of this the number of genuine early Christians would have been only a few.

Rebuttal #1: The Bible speaks about a falling away in the *end* times. Jehovah's Witnesses claim that we are living in the end times *now*. And remember, in order for a person to fall away he or she must have something to fall away from in the first place.

The Watchtower hierarchy claims that in 1919 God chose them to be "His sole channel of communication to this earth." At that time there were about 20,000 Jehovah's Witnesses. If one adds up the number of those who have joined the Watchtower organization over the years and compares it to the total growth, it is easy to see that at least one third of those who join eventually fall way. It seems to me that a one-third falling away is a high percentage! However, even with one third of the Jehovah's Witnesses falling away, they have grown from 20,000 in 1919 to four million by 1990, a period of seventy years. If there really was a large falling away in apostolic times as the Watchtower Society likes to intimate (though neither the Bible nor church history indicates this), it is very hard to believe that the Watchtower organization could do more evangelizing in seventy years than Jesus Christ and His twelve disciples!

The church that Jesus Christ started was a pure church. By its own admission, the Watchtower Society was almost completely pagan when it began. It has been and is still trying to get rid of these pagan practices. Its leaders claim to keep getting "new light" which is supposed to expose and correct the mistakes (paganism) of their earlier teachings. Of course this will never happen, because it is all built upon false precepts.

We know from the book of Revelation (written about 96 A.D.) that the true church was then still upon the earth. This would be about seventy years after the founding of the church. It is very hard for me to accept the fact that the pure church which Jesus Christ started with His twelve apostles could not have realized anywhere near 144,000 true conversions in seventy years. But if what the Watchtower says is correct, the early church could not have had more than 44,000 members—because the Watchtower Society had approximately 100,000 members prior to 1935 and all those were among the 144,000.

(You can press them on this point because it is very important. They have never thought about this, and it should be a help in opening their eyes to the unreliability of their teaching about the 144,000.)

The early church never taught that only 144,000 would go to heaven. In John 14:1–3 Jesus said that there were many dwelling places in heaven. (No restrictions here.) In John 17:24 Jesus prayed, "Father, I will that they also, whom thou hast given me, be with me where I am; that they may behold my glory, which thou hast given me: for thou lovedst me before the foundation of the world." Yes, Jesus requested of the Father that *all* believers go to heaven to be with Him. There is no indication that the number of believers in heaven might be restricted.

There is not one word, or even a hint, in the Gospels or Epistles that the number destined for heaven is restricted. There is nothing found in the writings of the church fathers either, that the number of those who could go to heaven would be restricted to just 144,000.

Since the Revelation of John was not written until 96 A.D., it is clear that for at least seventy years there was no teaching that only 144,000 would go to heaven. (And as we have seen, by 96 A.D. there were well over 144,000 who had become faithful believers.)

From Philippians 3:20–21 we know that these people looked forward to going to heaven:

> For our conversation [citizenship] is in heaven; from whence also we look for the Saviour, the Lord Jesus Christ: who shall change our vile body, that it may be fashioned like unto his glorious body, according to the working whereby he is able even to subdue all things unto himself

The Thessalonica Christians obviously looked forward to heaven. First Thessalonians 4:13–17 states:

> But I would not have you to be ignorant, brethren, concerning them which are asleep, that ye sorrow not, even as others which have no hope. For if we believe that Jesus died and rose again, even so them also which sleep in Jesus will God bring with him. For this we say unto you by the word of the Lord, that we which are alive and remain unto the coming of the Lord shall not prevent [precede] them which are asleep. For the Lord himself shall descend from heaven with a shout, with the voice of the archangel, and with the trump of God:

and the dead in Christ shall rise first: then we which are alive and remain shall be caught up together with them in the clouds, to meet the Lord in the air: and so shall we ever be with the Lord.

The Bible is clear as to what happens when the Lord returns to set up His kingdom. It says that the dead will rise first and go to heaven. (It does not say that the dead will gradually be raised during the 1000-year reign of Christ and given a second chance upon the earth. Revelation 20:5 states, "But the rest of the dead lived not again until the thousand years were finished.") It also states that those who are alive at His coming will meet the Lord in the clouds and then go back with Him to heaven and will ever be with the Lord. This is what is often called "the Rapture"—the "catching away." (The Bible nowhere indicates that at the time of Armageddon the saints alone will survive and continue on the earth; rather, it states that the saints will go into heaven to be with the Lord.)

Peter tells the many Christians he is writing to that they are to look forward to heaven, and it is certain because they are kept from falling by the power of God. He says:

Blessed be the God and Father of our Lord Jesus Christ, which according to his abundant mercy hath begotten us again unto a lively hope by the resurrection of Jesus Christ from the dead, to an inheritance incorruptible, and undefiled, and that fadeth not away, reserved in heaven for you, who are kept by the power of God through faith unto salvation ready to be revealed in the last time (1 Pet. 1:3–5).

Jude clearly taught the true believers that they would go to heaven and gave the reason for their assurance:

Now unto him that is able to keep you from falling, and to present you faultless before the presence of his glory with exceeding joy, to the only wise God our Saviour, be glory and majesty, dominion and power, both now and ever. Amen (Jude 24–25).

The Bible accurately relates to us the future state of the Old Testament saints who are in heaven. Hebrews states this in very plain language:

> By faith Abraham, when he was called to go out into a place which he should after receive for an inheritance, obeyed; and he went out, not knowing whither he went. By faith he sojourned in the land of promise, as in a strange country, dwelling in tabernacles with Isaac and Jacob, the heirs with him of the same promise: for he looked for a city which hath foundations, whose builder and maker is God (Heb. 11:8–10).
> These all died in faith, not having received the promises, but having seen them afar off, and were persuaded of them, and embraced them, and confessed that they were strangers and pilgrims on the earth. For they that say such things declare plainly that they seek a country. And truly, if they had been mindful of that country from whence they came out, they might have had opportunity to have returned. But now they desire a better country, that is, an heavenly: wherefore God is not ashamed to be called their God: for he hath prepared for them a city (Heb. 11:13–16).

God had promised Abraham, Isaac and Jacob the earthly land of Palestine. But they realized it was only for their earthly journey. They did not look forward to someday coming back to earth and living on the land God had promised. They looked forward to a city "whose builder and maker is God." (This can't be the new earth as described by the Watchtower Society, because the Jehovah's Witnesses themselves have to build the new earth and not God.) It is stated that heaven is a better country than the earth—and this is why these Old Testament saints looked forward to a heavenly country, which of course is heaven.

Jesus gave us a glimpse into the future and told us where Abraham, Isaac and Jacob would spend eternity: "And I [Jesus] say unto you, That many shall come from the east and west, and shall sit down with Abraham, and Isaac, and Jacob, in the kingdom of heaven" (Matt. 8:11).

So Abraham, Isaac and Jacob, along with others, looked forward to the kingdom of heaven and not a new earth.

David also had a heavenly hope. The words of David should be familiar to everyone. "Surely goodness and mercy shall follow me all the days of my life: and I will dwell in the house of the Lord [heaven] for ever" (Ps. 23:6).

(You only need to use as many of the following five questions under this heading as you feel necessary to get the point across.)

Question #2: As I mentioned before, there is absolutely no way for any of the 144,000 (if that is all who go to heaven) to be still alive in 1880. In fact, Charles Russell himself said that most of the 144,000 were chosen by the end of the first century, but now in the last days there were a few left of this "class," probably around 6000 to 9000, which were the remaining members to be chosen for the bride of Christ. He wrote in the *Zion's Watch Tower* (October and November, 1881, p. 3) that as of October 3, 1881, the number of chosen ones had been completed and no one could become a member of this class after this date. Here is what he actually wrote:

> The seven years which ended October 3, 1881, were years of favor during the presence, that of the living generation all of readiness of heart might become members of the little flock and enter into the joys of our Lord's presence. If our application of Scripture be correct, the "favor" has now ended, and in the language of the parable, "the door was shut"; and to those who have never fully consecrated and sacrificed self to God,

we cannot any longer hold out the great prize of our high calling, viz.; to be members of the Bride of Christ, joint heirs of Glory, Honor and Immortality.

I would like to know who told Charles Russell that there were between 6000 to 9000 openings left? This is something that could never be known from reading the Bible or studying history. It would have to come directly from God. Also, how did he come upon the date October 3, 1881? Apparently the Watchtower Society later decided that Charles Russell's application of Scripture was not correct because they left the door open for another 135,000 to 138,000. But how did they know?

(By the way, it is interesting to note that the Watchtower Society once taught that the "great crowd" was going to heaven, but that they "weren't quite good enough" to be part of the Bride of Christ.)

Somewhere along the line they expanded the number of openings in the "anointed class," but membership in the remnant was limited to Jehovah's Witnesses baptized before 1935. (These people didn't even have to go from door to door on a regular basis, but just had to be associated with the Society.) In 1935 it was announced that a "great crowd of other sheep" would remain on earth throughout eternity. (For details see *Life Everlasting in Freedom of the Sons of God*, 1966, p. 148, and *United in Worship of the Only True God*, 1983, p. 112.)

Response #2: (You probably won't get any.)

Question #3: One very, very important question comes to mind. If what the Watchtower Society said about the number being closed in 1935 was correct (though we have already seen that it was impossible for any openings to be left), how did they get this information? May I point out again that these are chosen by God, so He would be the only one to know exactly who they are and when the number was full. (Since it is an exact number, the time could not vary even by a few days.) Did God speak directly to Joseph Rutherford?

How did this information come down to man?

Response #3: (Probably none.)

Question #4: There is another piece of information concerning the 144,000 which needs to be answered. If it is true that membership in the anointed class was closed in 1935, it would be only logical that as the years continued the people began to die off and the number alive would show a steady decrease. This seemed to be true for many years, but the published figures on the remnant of the 144,000 from 1970 to 1983 show some interesting facts. (*The Orwellian World of Jehovah's Witnesses*, p. 144)

Year	Remnant of 144,000
1970	10,526
1971	10,384
1972	10,350
1973	10,523 (An increase of 173)
1974	10,723 (An increase of 200)
1975	10,550
1976	10,187
1977	10,080
1978	9,762
1979	9,727
1980	9,564
1981	9,601 (An increase of 37)
1982	9,529
1983	9,292

Even if there had been a few who fell away, and other people took their place, the exact number would not increase. It is very strange that the Watchtower Society allows for and, in fact, teaches that many people will fall away (actually about one third of its membership does so) but it allows for very, very few of the "anointed" to fall away!

Response #4: (None.)

Question #5: There is still another very mysterious problem that must be solved about the 144,000 if the Watchtower teaching is really true. The Society states that the 144,000 are the "worthy ones" appointed of God. In order for one to be considered for such a high calling, then, it would seem only logical that they would have to prove themselves by their "fruit." However, just about everything practiced by the Jehovah's Witnesses before 1935 is now considered pagan. For example:

- They voted and took part in government.
- Were allowed to participate in war.
- Could observe Christmas, birthdays, and other holidays.
- Were permitted to smoke.
- Were not against blood transfusions.
- Did not use the proper name for God.
- Did not have a proper organization.
- Believed that Jesus died on a cross.
- Were permitted to worship Jesus.
- Believed all Jehovah's Witnesses would go to heaven.
- Believed that the "higher powers" mentioned in Romans 13:1 referred to God and Christ.
- Believed that Christ's invisible return occurred in 1874.

I just can't comprehend why God would choose people with such pagan beliefs and practices to live and reign with Him! If what the Watchtower Society says about Proverbs 4:18 is true—that they are continually getting "new light" and the light is getting "lighter and lighter"—then it would seem to me that God would surely wait until the very end and choose those having the purest doctrines and practices to reign with Him!

Response #5: (None.)

Question #6: How do you explain the fact that the Watchtower Society teaches two different ways of salvation? John 3:16, 5:24, 10:28, and other verses which speak about having "eternal life" are said to apply only to the 144,000 "heavenly class." And they obtained this life without going from door to door but simply because they became Jehovah's Witnesses before 1935. While the "other sheep," the earthly class, can receive eternal life only after the end of the Millennium, and only if they "endure to the end"! Why do the *elite* gain eternal life so easily, yet the *flunkies* have to work so hard for their salvation?

Response #6: (Probably a perplexed look.)

Question #7: One last question on this subject. What will the 144,000 do after the 1000-year reign of Christ? The Watchtower Society plays down heaven. They ask the question, "What will you do in heaven?", implying that there will be nothing to do and it will not be an interesting place. The Society also teaches that after the 1000-year reign of Christ the kingdom is given to the Father. In other words, Christ is demoted from being ruler because there is nothing more for Him to do. Since the 144,000 reign only with Christ, then they also will have nothing to do. How do you solve this problem?

Response #7: (Probably none.)

BACKGROUND: The very foundation of the Watchtower Society is based on the fact that there are still some of the anointed class living today—because all the men on the governing body must be of the anointed class in order to understand the Bible and be "led by the spirit." As I have shown, there cannot be any of the anointed class left on earth today. This leaves the Watchtower Society without any authority, by their own definition of where their authority comes from.

NOTE: Questions regarding the 144,000 have prompted many Witnesses to leave the organization. This is a *very important area* to cover with them.

REQUESTING A FINANCIAL STATEMENT

Question: Any organization as large as the Society needs to issue regular financial statements. Please show me a current financial statement for the Watchtower Society.

Response: I can't give you a detailed financial statement because the Society does not issue one.

Rebuttal: Why don't they issue a financial statement? Approximately seventy percent of the Society's income comes from literature sales, yet they say that the donations for the literature cover only printing costs. Why is there no accountability in the area of finances?

PUNISHING THE WICKED

Question: The Watchtower Society teaches that all people will have the same end regardless of the kind of life they may have lived. Both the worst sinner and the best Jehovah's Witness will experience physical death—an obvious fact. But the Watchtower Society informs us that at death people are annihilated and cannot suffer conscious punishment or pain. The Society decares that "the wages of sin is death"—which is biblical—but it also declares that death is simply like falling asleep. And it states that everyone will be resurrected to enjoy life on the new earth. This does not seem fair, because the wicked are not punished and the righteous are not rewarded. Can you explain this teaching?

Response: (You probably will not get one.)

PUNISHING THE UNFAITHFUL WITNESS

Question: As we have discussed, the Society teaches that there is no real punishment for sins—unless a Witness does something wrong. A Witness can be in complete agreement with the Society; yet if he slips up in one area, he will be disfellowshipped, completely annihilated at death, and will not be resurrected to live on the new earth.

Some Witnesses have been disfellowshipped for disagreeing with the Society about one of its teachings. Later the Society has acknowledged that that specific teaching was wrong. However, I have never known the Society to apologize to the disfellowshipped person and reinstate him. Why is the Watchtower so severe with its members when the God of the Watchtower is so lenient regarding other sinners?

Response: (You probably won't get one.)

BUILDING THE NEW EARTH

BACKGROUND: The Watchtower Society teaches that everyone on earth will be destroyed during the battle of Armageddon except the Witnesses. This means that over five billion people will be killed and the four million surviving Jehovah's Witnesses will have the job of getting the earth ready for those who will be resurrected in the future.

This will obviously be a monumental task for these survivors. They will first need to dispose of the billions of bodies. Their books state that worms and birds will help with this task, but then the masses of worms and birds of carrion will need to be reduced to reasonable levels.

Once everything has been cleaned up, the Witnesses must build houses, plant gardens, and do the hundreds of other things that must be done before the resurrected ones appear. All this will have to be done by manual labor since all machinery will have been destroyed in the battle of Armageddon. Their books declare that it might take one hundred years to get the earth ready for God to begin resurrecting the dead.

(Until backed into a corner, the average Jehovah's Witness will equivocate and attempt to hide what they actually believe in this regard. To get them to admit these facts is like pulling eyeteeth. But be persistent.)

Question #1: Your description of the new earth sounds very inviting, but I have a problem understanding how the earth and its inhabitants are transformed from this present evil condition into the beautiful, paradise-like conditions you describe. Does something just go "poof" and this "new world order" suddenly appears?

Response #1: Well, it's not exactly like that. You see, before the new world order comes forth, Armageddon must occur.

Question #2: When will Armageddon occur?

Response #2: It will occur very soon.

Question #3: What happens at Armageddon?

Response #3: Just about all this world will be destroyed.

Question #4: How is this going to occur?

Response #4: (You probably will receive a vague answer, but their books and magazines contain vivid pictures of massive earthquakes, the earth swallowing up people, large buildings crumbling, fires destroying cities, and floods causing people to float down rivers. They also declare that people will kill each other, and those who do not die in these ways will be killed by God's angels.)

Question #5: Will everyone living upon this earth be killed at this time?

Response #5: Everyone but faithful Jehovah's Witnesses. (Your respondents might be vague, but this is what they believe and teach.)

Question #6: How will it be possible that only Jehovah's Witnesses survive when everyone else will be killed?

Response #6: Jehovah in some miraculous way will protect us.

Question #7: You mean that Jehovah's Witnesses will live through this horrible disaster, witnessing these people being killed, and will have to listen to the blood-curdling screams as people die in agonizing pain?

Response #7: I imagine that will be the case.

Question #8: After all this awful destruction, how is the "new world order" going to come about?

Response #8: (If they are honest with you, they will explain that the four-and-a-half million Jehovah's Witnesses must completely rebuild this earth, so that it becomes a paradise looking like the pictures contained in their publications.)

Question #9: It seems to me that the first thing the surviving Jehovah's Witnesses will have to do is to get rid of the five billion dead bodies lying all around! How is this going to be done, since dead bodies begin to decay and stink in just a day or so?

Response #9: Worms and birds are going to eat them up.

Question #10: You mean the first thing that the surviving Jehovah's Witnesses must do is stand around and watch the worms and birds eat those dead bodies?

Response #10: I guess so.

Question #11: This doesn't sound like it would be very enjoyable!

Response #11: We will endure for Jehovah's sake.

Question #12: After the worms and birds have devoured all that flesh, you will still have to dispose of the skeletons, won't you?

Response #12: Apparently so.

Question #13: The Watchtower publications picture everyone as living in beautiful homes on the new earth, with enough land for family gardens. But first the destroyed buildings must be gotten rid of. How is this going to be done, since all powered machinery will have been destroyed?

Response #13: I don't really know.

Question #14: Apparently the survivors will have to dig deep holes manually and bury all the rubble. Is this right?

Response #14: I don't really know. (Note: They should know, if they have been a Jehovah's Witness for any length of time, because on the back cover of the October 8, 1991, *Awake* magazine there is a picture of the destroyed earth and people with wheelbarrows, shovels and rakes cleaning up the debris.)

Question #15: How are they going to get a foot of topsoil back on the land where the buildings were torn down, since they will have no trucks and few passable roads?

Response #15: I don't know.

Question #16: How can so few people build sufficient houses for the billions of people who are to be resurrected?

Response #16: You need to realize that a group of Jehovah's Witnesses can now build a new Kingdom Hall in two days.

Question #17: Yes, but since this old system will be destroyed, there will be no lumberyards where you can buy lumber, cement, and other necessary building materials. This is something you will have to accomplish from scratch. In many places, trees are not available and will need to be transported long distances. How will this material be obtained?

Response #17: I don't know.

Question #18: These homes will need furniture and the people will need clothing. Where will you get these, since there will be no factories?

Response #18: I guess we must make all this.

Question #19: Who is going to live on this new earth that the Witnesses must work so hard to create?

Response #19: Nearly all the people who have ever lived.

Question #20: You mean that God is going to destroy all the wicked people on the earth, have the Jehovah's Witnesses work hard to rebuild the earth, and then He will resurrect these wicked people to enjoy the beautiful conditions the Jehovah's Witnesses have created?

Response #20: I really don't know.

Question #21: When will God start resurrecting these people to dwell on this beautiful earth that the Witnesses have to create?

Response #21: I don't know.

Question #22: How can the Jehovah's Witnesses enjoy the new living conditions if they have to continue working to build homes and make all the other things necessary for the billions of people who will be resurrected?

Response # 22: You need to understand that it will be a great joy to work for Jehovah.

Question #23: Will the people who are resurrected upon this earth be perfect?

Response #23: They will have paid for their sins at death but will not yet have learned how to be in conformity with God's will.

Question #24: Who is going to teach these billions of people how to be in conformity to God's will?

Response #24: This will be the privilege of the Jehovah's

Witnesses.

Question #25: In other words, you will not only be busy rebuilding the earth, but you will be very busy teaching! I don't think you will have much free time. And what happens to the people who do not respond to this education process?

Response #25: They will be annihilated.

Question #26: Then you will have death during this period of time?

Response #26: I guess so.

Question #27: Since your books state that during this time people will not grow old and die, how does Christ get rid of these wicked people?

Response #27: We are not quite sure.

Question #28: The only possible way I would know for them to be disposed of is for God to "zap" them. Would you say that this is right?

Response #28: I really can't answer you.

Question #29: I understand that you teach that there will be no funeral parlors or graveyards in the Millennium, so who is going to bury these people and where?

Response #29: I don't know.

Question #30: Would I be right in saying that this new earth will be a far from perfect place because many people will have to keep digging up their yards to bury these dead bodies?

Response #30: (I don't think you will get one.)

Question #31: Am I to believe that it will be a wonderful thing to survive Armageddon, get rid of all the dead bodies and bones, clean up all this awful destruction, and then work extremely hard to build a beautiful earth so that all the wicked people who have ever lived can be resurrected and enabled to enjoy what the Witnesses have worked so hard for?

Response #31: (If you get any kind of any answer, I think it will be a weak reply.)

LEARNING ABOUT THE SOCIETY'S HISTORY

BACKGROUND: The Witnesses do not like to discuss the history of the Watchtower Society because there have been so many changes in their teachings. The Society does not tell its followers the truth about these changes. By asking the following questions on the history of the Watchtower movement you can help them to realize that their doctrines are built not upon a solid foundation but on the changing ideas of men. Most Witnesses do not know the accurate history of the movement, so you are likely to get varied responses. For this reason I will state the facts—but you might get a different answer, or none at all.

Question #1: In what year was the Watchtower organization begun?

Fact #1: It was started in 1879.

Question #2: Was the organization started by one man or by a group of men?

Fact #2: It was started by one man, Charles Russell.

Question #3: The Watchtower Society claims that it is "the sole channel of God's communication to the earth." On what basis did Charles Russell make such a claim? Did Russell get revelations directly from heaven telling him what to teach?

Fact #3: They intimate that he did—stating that he was "guided by God." However, it is hard for them to claim that Russell got revelations directly from heaven because he made so many mistakes, causing changes to be made.

Question #4: The Watchtower Society says that it is different from every other group on earth. This difference is used to prove that it is God's only channel of communication to earth. What was the distinctive teaching of Charles Russell that no one else had?

Fact #4: Just about everything Charles Russell taught he borrowed from someone else, so he did not have any distinctives.

Question #5: Did any of Charles Russell's teachings

ever have to be changed? Did Russell make any predictions that did not come true?

Fact #5: Most of Russell's teachings have been altered. Russell falsely predicted that Christ would return and the present world system would end in 1914. Charles Russell was an ordinary man who did not have any divinely communicated truth.

Question #6: Does the Watchtower Society proudly acknowledge Charles Russell as the founder of the Society?

Fact #6: No. They mention Charles Russell in their books but they do not hold him up as their champion, because the Society itself realizes the many mistakes he made. They downplay Russell's role in the Society today, though at first he *was* the Society.

Question #7: Have you personally read any of Charles Russell's works in their entirety?

Fact #7: Very few Witnesses have read any of Russell's books or writings in their entirety. In fact, the Society no longer sells Charles Russell's books because of the many mistakes and changes. They quote Russell in their publications, but most quotes are taken out of context.

Question #8: How long did Charles Russell remain at the head of the Watchtower Society?

Fact #8: He was the head of the organization until he died on October 31, 1916.

Question #9: Who became the president after Charles Russell's death? On what basis did he get this position?

Fact #9: Joseph Rutherford (also known as Judge Rutherford) was the second president of the Society. They will not tell you that there was a real power struggle for the presidency and many members left at this time.

Question #10: Were any changes made in the Watchtower Society when Rutherford took control?

Fact #10: Many changes were made. Rutherford dismissed all those who opposed him. One of the most noticeable changes was in the interpretation of Romans 13:1, "Let every soul be subject unto the higher powers. For there is no power but of God: the powers that be are ordained of God." Russell had taught that this referred to earthly governments. Rutherford said that it meant Jehovah God and Christ. Many followers were disfellowshipped because they would not accept this new teaching. After Rutherford's death the Society once again taught that Romans 13:1 referred to earthly governments. This is one of many instances where people have been disfellowshipped for believing the right interpretation.

One lasting change made under Rutherford was his declaration in 1931 that "Jehovah" was the exclusive name for God. The Witnesses will condemn you if you do not use the name "Jehovah" for God. However, they did not use it during the organization's first fifty years.

Question #11: Did Joseph Rutherford set dates for Christ's return?

Fact #11: Joseph Rutherford first said that Christ would return in 1925. When this proved wrong, he changed his prediction and said that Christ's return would occur around 1940.

Question #12: How long was Joseph Rutherford head of the Society?

Fact #12: Joseph Rutherford died in 1942 at Beth-Sarim (House of Princes) in San Diego, California. He had this beautiful house built in 1930 to provide a home for many of the Old Testament princes. He taught that Abraham, Isaac, Jacob, and others would soon be awakened to come back to live on earth. Rutherford spent most of his later years there; and upon his death, the property was to be deeded to the princes. Of course, they never returned to live there, and the property has now been sold.

Question #13: Who took over the Society after the death of Rutherford?

Fact #13: He was quickly and quietly replaced by his former right-hand man, Nathan Knorr. Knorr was more efficient than Rutherford, but less charismatic. Under Knorr's leadership, the present system of going from door to door selling books and magazines was highly polished. During his time, the number of followers greatly increased.

Question #14: Were any changes made under the leadership of Knorr?

Fact #14: Knorr changed the interpretation of Romans 13:1 back to the governments of this world. Up until his time, it was taught that Christ's invisible return took place in 1874. That date was eventually changed to 1914, where it remains today. In the latter years of Nathan Knorr's rule, he was forced to accept a governing body. Some top Witnesses were against one-man rule, so they established a group of leaders. This group originally had fifteen men. Since then, four have been dismissed and labeled as apostates, and several have died. Most of these vacancies have been filled. However, the Society is very secretive about their governing body. Very few Jehovah's Witnesses know the names of the men on the governing body.

Question #15: After Knorr died, who became president of the Watchtower Society?

Fact #15: In 1977 Frederick W. Franz became the president. He had been the vice-president. This was the least dramatic change in the Society's leadership, because of the governing body.

Question #16: What changes were made after Franz became president?

Fact #16: After Franz became leader they abandoned the ban on human organ transplants. Before Franz became president he prophesied that the end of the 6000 years of man's existence upon this earth would come in October 1975. Armageddon would occur, causing the destruction of this earth and the beginning of the 1000-year reign of Christ. Until 1980, the Society denied that they had made such a prophecy. They said that their followers were teaching this on their own, apparently forgetting that Witnesses are not allowed to express their own opinions.

A great exodus of Witnesses occurred when the 1975 prophecy didn't come true. Many Witnesses had sold everything they owned. They went door-to-door full time while living off the proceeds of the sale of their property. When the world did not end, they had to make a new start in life. The Society encouraged the Witnesses in the sale of their possessions. However, when the prediction proved false, the Society condemned the action of its followers. The Society would accept no responsibility in this matter.

After the storm over the false prophecy ended, the Society began growing again. Most of this growth is occurring in countries other than America.

Question #17: Who is the current president of the Watchtower Society?

Fact #17: Milton G. Henschel became the fifth Watchtower president on December 30, 1992.

Question #18: The Watchtower Society says it is directed by God, yet many changes in what they teach have had to be made over the years. If the Society truly had divine guidance, why have so many mistakes been made? Surely God would get things right the first time!

Fact #18: They are not being led by God. They will admit that they make mistakes but claim that the changes show that they are "making progress."

Question #19: Can you tell me what teachings are one hundred percent from Jehovah God and will never need changing, and what teachings are from the leadership and probably will be changed at some point? I want a pure religion whose teachings will never change. I don't find this in the Watchtower Society. The teachings have changed so much in the last one hundred years that I am sure that they will continue to change in the future. How can the Society claim to be Jehovah's exclusive earthly organization when it cannot give me assurance that its current teachings are the truth?

Fact #19: They can't give any proof that they are God's divinely appointed organization nor can they give any assurance that their teachings will not change.

Question #20: Because the Society's teachings change

so frequently, wouldn't it be better to wait as long as possible to join the Society? It seems that the longer a person waits, the purer the Society's teaching is likely to be.

Fact #20: Their teachings are not becoming any more "pure" but, in reality, they are continuing to add more and more false teachings.

PAYING FOR SINS

Question: According to the Society, people pay the penalty for their sins when they die—since "the wages of sin is death" (Rom. 6:23). These people will get a fresh start on the new earth because they have paid for their sins. However, the Witnesses who survive Armageddon have not died, so they have not paid for their sins. How will these Witnesses pay for their sins?

Response: (Since most Witnesses have never thought about this, you probably will not get an answer.)

CHANGING BELIEFS

BACKGROUND: The Society has a list of teachings which they claim shows that they are Jehovah God's approved organization. They are:

TODAY	BEFORE 1930
They do not vote or get involved in government.	They could vote and could be involved in government
They are against war.	They were allowed to join the army, go to war, and work at military installations. The ban on these practices began in 1940.
They don't observe Christ-	They observed birthdays,

TODAY	BEFORE 1930
mas, birthdays, and other holidays which they consider pagan.	Christmas and other holidays.
They use the name "Jehovah" exclusively for God.	They did not use the name "Jehovah" exclusively for God. This practice started in 1931.
They have an organization.	They said that they were not an organization.
They have a theocratic government ruled by a governing body.	They did not have a governing body. This did not begin until the early 1970's.
They look forward to paradise on the new earth.	They believed that all Jehovah's Witnesses were part of the "anointed class" who would go to heaven. The teaching about the "other sheep" living in paradise on the new earth was not put forth until after 1935.
They are against blood transfusions.	They could receive blood transfusions. The ban on transfusions did not begin until 1945.
They believe that Jesus died on a torture stake.	They believed that Jesus died on a cross. They have a picture of Jesus hanging on the cross in their 1921 publication, *The Harp of God*. Rutherford writes about Jesus dying on the cross in his 1928 book, *Reconciliation*.

TODAY	BEFORE 1930
They believed that Christ returned invisibly in 1914.	They believed that Christ's invisible return occurred in 1874.
They do not worship Jesus.	They worshiped Jesus even though they did not believe that He is truly God.
They believe that the authorities mentioned in Romans 13:1 are earthly kingdoms and rulers.	They believed that the authorities mentioned in Romans 13:1 are God and Christ.
They are against smoking.	They were not against smoking. The ban on smoking began in 1975. (They still see nothing wrong in consuming alcoholic beverages.)
They claim they are the only group that has gone to many nations of the world preaching the kingdom. (Even though they are in about two hundred countries, I have never heard of them going to an uncivilized tribe to learn their language, translate the Bible, and then teach the people.)	They had not gone into very many countries of the world with their teachings.

Question #1: If the Society's teachings are proof that it is right, why are all these teachings different from what was believed sixty years ago?

Response #1: You need to understand that we are continually getting "new light" and are making progress.

Rebuttal #1: The things that you label pagan today are the things that you used to teach as truth. If these things are pagan, then the Watchtower Society was a pagan organization in 1930!

Question #2: If the "fruits" they pointed to sixty years ago are now considered "pagan," then the early Watchtower Society was a pagan organization! Why would God choose an organization which held so many pagan beliefs to be "His sole channel of communication to this earth"?

Response #2: (Probably none.)

MAKING MISTAKES

BACKGROUND: The Watchtower Society feels that mistakes are acceptable so long as they are willing to admit them and have a desire to correct them. I do not think I would like a doctor who practiced under this principle. Suppose a doctor never went to medical school, but instead decided to learn medicine by trial and error. How long would people continue to go to such a doctor? A person would not normally put his physical life into the hands of a doctor who learned by trial and error, so why should anyone put his spiritual life into the hands of a religion that is being developed by trial and error?

Question: The Watchtower Society presents its teachings as "true light." All Witnesses must believe these things or be disfellowshipped. However, the Society frequently says that it has received "new light" which makes the old teachings wrong. They say that this is acceptable so long as they admit their mistakes and desire to make progress. How can this be?

Response: All mankind is imperfect; so are Jehovah's Witnesses. The apostles Paul and Peter both made mistakes— serious ones—but they continued making Christian progress in humility. No man on this earth is perfect, nor is any religious organization.

Rebuttal: Peter and Paul made mistakes as men, but

they never made mistakes in their inspired writings. We never find where they had to go back and correct something that they wrote under the inspiration of the Holy Spirit. The Watchtower Society claims that they write under divine guidance, yet they have made many changes to those writings over the years.

It is easy for the Society to admit that they make mistakes, but that does not help those who have suffered physically and/or emotionally from those mistakes. Let me give you several examples:

• Many Witnesses were injured or killed during the sixty years they were allowed to go to war. Many innocent people were killed by the Witnesses who went to war.

• Probably many Witnesses contacted smallpox during the years the Watchtower Society prohibited vaccinations.

• Witnesses died who could have lived if they had been allowed to have organ transplants.

• Witnesses who are disfellowshipped suffer great emotional anguish because they are completely cut off from family and friends. Many have suffered this anguish needlessly because the Society has been in error. However, the Society does nothing to rectify these errors, and the people remain disfellowshipped.

Don't you think the Society should check out a matter thoroughly and be absolutely sure it is correct before teaching it? This would prevent needless suffering.

RECEIVING NEW LIGHT

BACKGROUND: In the preceding section, we looked at some of the mistakes the Society has made over the years. The Society says they made changes as they received "new light." They use Proverbs 4:18 to explain this. The verse says, "But the path of the righteous ones is like the bright light that is getting lighter and lighter until the day is firmly established" (NWT).

The Society claims that its teachings come directly from God. The *1939 Yearbook of Jehovah's Witnesses* states: "It should be expected that the Lord would have a means of communication to his people on the earth, and he has clearly shown that the magazine called *The Watchtower* is used for that purpose" (p. 185).

Frederick Franz, who was vice-president of the organization at that time, gave the following answers in a court case in 1943 (*Olin Moyle v. Watch Tower Bible and Truct Society*):

> Q. At any rate, Jehovah God is now the editor of the paper, is that right?
> A. He is today the editor of the paper.
> Q. How long has He been editor of the paper?
> A. Since its inception He has been guiding it.

During the same court case, Nathan Knorr, then president of the organization, gave these answers:

> Q. But you don't make any such statement, that you are subject to correction, in your Watch Tower papers, do you?
> A. Not that I recall.
> Q. In fact, it is set forth directly as God's Word, isn't it?
> A. Yes, as His Word.
> Q. Without any qualification whatsoever?
> A. That is right.

In the book *Vindication*, a Watchtower publication, it explains how "new light" is received from God.

> These angels are invisible to human eyes and are there to carry out the orders of the Lord. No doubt they first hear the instruction which the Lord issues to his remnant and then these invisible messengers pass such

instruction on to the remnant. The facts show that the angels of the Lord with him at his temple have been thus rendering service unto the remnant since 1919 (Vol. 3, p. 250).

If the above statement really is true, since the "new light" needs to be changed so often there are two possible conclusions that a person can come to. Either, the information which is supposed to come from heaven is not being correctly received, something like a telephone with a poor connection; or, the information which is supposed to come from heaven is being correctly received but is deliberately being changed by the men on the governing body.

Though the Jehovah'sWitnesses continually talk about this "new light" they do not have the faintest idea of how it is arrived at by the governing body. (By majority vote.) There are two possible sources of light: God (1 John 1:5) and Satan (2 Cor. 11:14). Questions on this subject can be very helpful in causing Witnesses to do some serious thinking.

Question #1: The Watchtower Society sometimes writes about receiving "new light." Would you say that this "new light" is from God?

Response #1: Yes.

Question #2: Is there any other possible source of light?

Response #2: Yes. Satan.

Question #3: Would you please explain the process—how this "new light" comes down from God and is received by the men on the governing body.

Response #3: I am not exactly sure.

Question #4: Would it be safe to say that since this "new light" comes from God, it is absolute truth and never changes?

Response #4: No. Sometimes adjustments need to be made.

Question #5: How can you say that it comes from God if it can change?

Response #5: You have to realize that the men on the

governing body are human men and they do make mistakes.

Question #6: Then this "new light" does not come directly from God. The men on the governing body decide what they think God might want, but often they are mistaken. Would you agree with this?

Response #6: Well, they do make mistakes, but at least they admit them.

Question #7: Then you are telling me that this "new light" does not come directly from God but from the governing body?

Response #7: I guess that would be right.

Question #8: How do the men on the governing body figure out what they are to present as "new light" from God?

Response #8: I don't know.

Question #9: I can understand truth building upon truth, but it will never change. However, if this "new light" can and does change, then it could not have been the truth in the first place. Wouldn't you say that is right?

Response #9: I told you that we admit our mistakes and make adjustments.

Question #10: As you have admitted, the governing body has made many mistakes. Therefore, when this "new light" is presented, arc you free to choose if you want to follow it or not?

Response #10: No. We must go along with the new light.

Question #11: I am confused. You talk about this "new light" but admit that it really does not come from God but from the governing body. However, you do not know how they decide what to put forth as "new light." Yet you have to be in complete subjection to the governing body even while knowing that in the future the "light" might change and that the error could be harmful to many people. For example, in 1967 the Watchtower Society forbade its followers to receive organ transplants, but in 1980 it reversed its decision. During those thirteen years some people probably died and others went blind. Could you please explain this to me in a way that I can understand your thinking?

Response #11: (I don't think you will get one.)

TEACHING DURING THE MILLENNIUM

Question: The Watchtower teaches that all people, except Jesus Christ and disfellowshipped Jehovah's Witnesses, will be resurrected. These resurrected people will have been made perfect because their own deaths paid for their sins. However, most of these people did not accept the teachings of the Society during this life. Therefore, they will need to be taught these things during the Millennium. I understand that they will be given one hundred to five hundred years to conform to Jehovah's will as taught by the Society. If they refuse, they will be annihilated.

The Society teaches that the Witnesses will be doing the teaching. But the question is: What will they be teaching? The teachings of the Watchtower Society have changed greatly over its one hundred years of existence. The Society claims that the dead don't know anything, so, obviously, those Witnesses who have died will not know about all the changes that have been made. Thus, they will be resurrected with outdated beliefs. The Witnesses on the new earth will not be unified in their beliefs. What plan does the Society have to solve this problem?

Response: (Probably none.)

INVESTIGATING THE SOCIETY

The following questions will show that the Witness you are talking to did not obey the Bible at 1 John 4:1, where we are told to test a religion before we join. (I will not present responses to these questions because most likely the J.W. will have to say "no" to most of them, or he will give a very vague answer.)

Question #1: How did you investigate the Watchtower Society before you joined it? Did you read books both for and against the Society to help you judge it accurately?

Question #2: Had you read the Bible in its entirety?

Question #3: If the context of a verse is ignored, people can prove anything they wish from it. To prevent this problem, did you read the Bible passages found in the Watchtower publications *in context* to make sure they were applied accurately?

Question #4: Were you well acquainted with the teachings of any Bible-believing, gospel-preaching church before you began to study with the Witnesses?

Question #5: What was the process that you used to test the Watchtower organization before you joined?

Question #6: Have you ever checked the quotations the Society uses from other sources to see whether or not they are taken out of context?

FALLING AWAY

BACKGROUND: Between 1970 and 1980, approximately one-third of the Watchtower membership was disfellowshipped. (Anyone who leaves the Society for whatever reason is considered to have been disfellowshipped.) The Watchtower teaches that all disfellowshipped Witnesses will receive the most severe punishment—eternal annihilation at the end of this life. They will not be resurrected in the future to enjoy life on the new earth. However, they teach that people who never become Jehovah's Witnesses will be resurrected and given a second chance.

Question: If the Watchtower Society's teachings are correct, it seems that it would be best not to become a Jehovah's Witness in this life. If a person does not become a Witness, he has a one hundred percent chance of getting to the new earth. However, if he becomes a Witness, history proves he has only a sixty-seven percent chance of getting to the new earth and a thirty-three percent chance of being eternally annihilated. Can you explain this?

Response: (They may try to deny that thirty-three percent of the Witnesses fall away, but ask them to check the records of the Society.)

FINDING THE TRUE CHURCH

Question #1: Was the original church that Christ founded the true and pure church?

Rebuttal #1 (If they answer "yes"): If the church Christ founded was the true church, it would not be necessary for God to give any more light. All a person would need to do is study the doctrines and teachings of the original church.

Since Christ established the true church, the 144,000 quota was filled long before Charles Russell was born. Therefore, the leaders of the Watchtower Society cannot possibly be members of the 144,000. Yet the Society teaches that these men must be members of the 144,000. This really complicates matters.

Rebuttal #2 (If they answer "no"): If Christ did not found the true church, then He founded a pagan church. And if the leaders of the Society continually need to get more light, then the Society was originally founded on pagan practices. Why did God wait for over 1800 years to begin to reveal accurately what is in the Bible? And why did God not reveal everything at once? If Jehovah God is behind the Watchtower Society, why does it still have so much darkness in it? This doesn't make sense.

LEARNING ABOUT THE GOVERNING BODY

BACKGROUND: While the Watchtower Society claims to be "God's only agency on earth," much of what they claim God told them has come from the members of the governing body. If it had come from God, the teachings would have been correct from the beginning. Most Witnesses know very little about the governing body. The following questions are built upon this fact. Their answers are likely to be a series of "I'm not sure."

Question #1: How many members are on the governing body?

Fact #1: Originally, there were fifteen members. There are about thirteen today.

Question #2: What are the names of the men on the governing body?

Fact #2: Milton Henschel is the president; but even though the other members might be mentioned individually from time to time, they rarely give a complete list. Very few Witnesses will be able to name more than a few, if they can do that.

Question #3: How were the men on the governing body chosen?

Fact #3: The process is not made known. In reality, it is a self-perpetuating committee.

Question #4: What are the qualifications needed for being on the governing body?

Fact #4: No information is given concerning this, other than the necessity of being one of the 144,000.

Question #5: Inasmuch as the Jehovah's Witnesses have spread all over the world, I would assume that there are men on the governing body from Asia, South America, Africa, Europe, etc., so that all nations might be equally represented. Is this true?

Fact #5: All the men on the governing body are white Americans.

Question #6: It seems to me that God could be a little more fair! Would you explain the reason for only having white Americans?

Fact #6: The Society is not interested in equal representation and wants to keep complete control of the organization in the hands of its self-perpetuating governing body—made up entirely of white American males.

Question #7: For almost ninety years the Society was run by the president, who had complete authority. When was the change made to a governing body, and why?

Fact #7: The Witnesses are told that they have always

had a governing body, so most do not know it came into existence in the early 1970's.

INTERPRETING THE BIBLE

BACKGROUND: Before one attempts to discuss any Bible verses with a Witness, it is important to get the J.W. to admit that they are not allowed to interpret the Bible on their own. It is a fact that the Society first develops its doctrines and then attempts to find Bible verses to prove them. To do this, it has had to take many verses out of context and ignore other verses on the subject. Witnesses are not allowed to explore the Bible on their own because the Society realizes that they will lose them if they do. The following questions should help Witnesses admit that they are blindly following the Society's interpretations.

Question #1: Can a person read the Bible on his own and come up with the truth?

Response #1: No.

Question #2: Why?

Response #2: Acts 8:31 says, "How can I [understand], except some man should guide me?"

Rebuttal #2: The Ethiopian eunuch was reading the Bible. Philip expounded the Bible and did not use books put out by some organization. It is important to notice who it was that Philip pointed the Ethiopian eunuch to. Acts 8:35 reads, "Then Philip opened his mouth, and began at the same scripture, and preached unto him Jesus." I don't think Jehovah's Witnesses start with Jesus! The Bible states in Acts 8:39, "The Spirit of the Lord caught away Philip, [so] that the eunuch saw him no more: and he went on his way rejoicing." When Philip was taken away, the eunuch was left with just his Bible. Isn't it striking that God should have Luke record this particular incident for us!

Question #3: Do you always read the verses in context?

Response #3: Yes. (They are not telling the truth, because they very seldom do. And if you try to get them to do it, they are likely to say it is a waste of time to read so many verses.)

Question #4: When trying to learn what the Bible says on a matter, do you read all the verses on that subject and come to a conclusion only after comparing them?

Response #4: (If they are truthful they will answer "no," but you can't always depend upon them telling the truth. J.W.'s are not willing to go to the trouble of finding all the verses on the subject at hand and comparing them carefully. When they get an idea, they try to find a verse or part of a verse that seems to prove what they have already decided. Then they ignore other verses on that subject.)

Question #5: How do you reach your conclusions?

Response #5: We do not come to conclusions ourselves. The organization does that for us.

Question #6: Why did God allow only one man to interpret the Bible for almost eighty years and then suddenly switch to fifteen or so men? Why are all the men Americans? And why did God wait for almost 1,900 years before finding someone for this job? Surely He could have found someone to do the job before then—especially since the governing body makes so many mistakes!

Response #6: (None.)

Question #7: The Society teaches that it is the only one that has the right to interpret the Bible. On what valid basis can the leaders make this claim?

Response #7: (It will be hard for them to give a convincing reply to this question.)

Question #8: How do I know that what you are telling me about the Bible is true, since the Society has made so many mistakes?

Response #8: We are making progress.

Question #9: Can you give me a guarantee that what you are telling me today won't be changed tomorrow by "new light"?

Response #9: No.

Question #10: Then there is a good possibility that

some things you are teaching right now will turn out to be false teachings in the future. I thought you were against pagan teaching, but you have often taught pagan ideas. How can you continue to present your teachings as truth when you know there is a very good possibility that they will need to be changed in the future?

Response #10: (None)

After you have gone through a sufficient number of these questions you will have caused the Jehovah's Witness you are conversing with to do some serious thinking and begin to question his religion. Now you ought to be able to present the gospel in a clear way, using the Bible, without much conflict. The next chapter will explain how you can present the gospel in a thought-provoking way.

CHAPTER EIGHT

HOW TO LEAD THE WITNESS TO CHRIST

In 1 John 4:1–3 we are told that we should test every religion to see if it be from God. Tell the Witness that you would like him to compare what you believe *with the Bible alone.* Since you have listened to his beliefs, request his cooperation while you explain what you believe.

NOTE: The New World Translation of the Bible by the Watchtower Society is greatly corrupted when it comes to their major doctrines. However, most of the other verses have *not* been doctored, even though their translation is rather awkward reading. Let the Witness use his own Bible if he wishes while you explain what you believe. This will prove to him that the New World Translation does not agree with what the Society teaches! J.W.'s have a hard time ignoring the truth when it is presented to them from their own Bible.

The Witness is undoubtedly familiar with the Watchtower publication *You Can Live Forever in Paradise on Earth.* In Chapter 3, "Your Religion Really Matters," pp. 29–31, it says:

> Since God does not approve of all religions, we need to ask: "Am I worshiping God in the way that he approves?" How can we know if we are? It is not any man, but God, who is the judge of what is true worship. So if our worship is to be acceptable to God, it must be firmly rooted in God's Word of truth, the Bible. We should feel the same way as the Bible writer who said: "Let God be found true, though every man be found a liar."—Romans 3:3–4.
>
> . . . So if we want God's approval, it is necessary that we make sure that what we believe is in agreement

with the teachings of the Bible.

Since many religions today are not doing God's will, we cannot simply assume that the teachings of the religious organization we are associated with are in agreement with God's Word. The mere fact that the Bible is used by a religion does not of itself prove that all the things it teaches and practices are in the Bible. It is important that we ourselves examine whether they are or not. . . . The religion that is approved by God must agree in every way with the Bible; it will not accept certain parts of the Bible and reject other parts—2 Timothy 3:16.

Acts 17:11 says, "These were more noble than those in Thessalonica, in that they received the word with all readiness of mind, and searched the scriptures daily, whether those things were so."

Do not hurry through this section. Make sure that the Witness understands the point of each verse before you move on to the next verse. If there is any question about what a verse means, read it in the context of the surrounding passage.

Answer questions about your beliefs, but try not to let him get you off onto other subjects. Tell him you will be happy to discuss those other subjects after you have finished explaining what you believe.

SIN. I believe that man was born in sin; man has a sin nature; man has knowingly committed sin; and man is responsible for his own actions.

When the Bible speaks of sin, it includes: unthankfulness, selfishness, self-centeredness, pride, boasting, hypocrisy, covetousness, maliciousness, jealousy, deceitfulness, backbiting, idol worship, wrathfulness, hating, lying, gossiping, causing divisions, lust, sensuality, fornication, adultery, drunkenness, stealing, evil thoughts, etc. (See Psalm 51:5; 58:3; Isa. 53:6; 64:6; Jer. 17:9; Matt. 15:18–19; Rom. 1:24–32;

3:10–23; 1 Tim. 1:15; 2 Tim. 3:1–5; Titus 3:3; James 4:17.)

SIN CAUSES SPIRITUAL AND PHYSICAL DEATH.
Sin must be punished. (See Gen. 2:17; Rom. 6:23; Eph. 2:1–9; Col. 2:13; James 5:20; 1 John 3:14.)

SIN SEPARATES MAN FROM GOD. (See Gen. 3:8–10; Isa. 59:2; Eph. 2:11–13.)

WE CANNOT AVOID SPIRITUAL DEATH AND GAIN ETERNAL LIFE THROUGH OUR OWN EFFORTS.
Dead men can't work. Being good is not enough; we must be declared righteous by God. (See Rom. 4:5; 11:6; Gal. 2:16; Eph. 2:8–9; Titus 3:5–6.)

CHRIST SHED HIS BLOOD FOR ALL OF MY SINS— NOT JUST THOSE THAT I INHERITED FROM ADAM.
(See John 3:16; Acts 3:19; 10:43; 13:38; 26:18; 1 Cor. 15:1–4; 2 Cor. 5:21; Gal. 1:4; Eph. 1:7; 2:13; Col. 1:14; Heb. 1:3; 1 Peter 1:18–19; 2:24; 3:18; 1 John 1:9; 3:5; Rev. 1:5; 7:14.)

WE MUST ACCEPT CHRIST AS OUR OWN PER-SONAL SAVIOR. (See John 3:36; 5:24; Acts 4:10–12; 16:31; Rom. 10:9–13.)

TO BECOME SONS OF GOD, WE MUST BE BORN OF GOD. When we trust Christ as our personal Savior, all of our sins are immediately forgiven because of the merit of His blood. Once we become children of God, we will always be children of God. As a child of God, our sin will hinder our fellowship with God, but it will never cancel our salvation. (See John 1:12–13; 3:3; 2 Cor. 5:17; 1 Peter 1:23; 1 John 3:1–2; 5:1,4.)

WE ARE SAVED TO A LIFE OF HOLINESS. We should no longer live according to the desires of our old nature. (See Rom. 6:1–2; 2 Cor. 5:17; 7:1; Eph. 1:4; 4:24; 1 Thess.

2:12; 4:1–17; Heb. 12:14; 1 Peter 1:15–16; 2 Peter 3:11.)

EXAMPLES OF HOLINESS. (See Rom. 12:10; Gal. 5:22–23; Eph, 4:2–3, 29, 31–32; Phil. 2:3–4; Col. 3:12–14; James 1:19–20; 3:16–18; 1 Peter 2:1; 3:7–9.)

WE HAVE A WORKING FAITH. A Christian does not need works to gain salvation or earn merit for himself. Instead, he works because he wants to please God. (See 2 Cor. 9:8; Eph. 2:10; Col. 1:10; 2 Thess. 2:16–17; Titus 2:7, 14.)

CHRISTIANS CAN BE ASSURED THAT THEY HAVE ETERNAL LIFE. Just as parents protect and care for their children, so God protects and cares for His children. Some people say it is possible for a person to turn away from Christ. But it is hard for me to understand how anyone who has known the wonderful salvation there is in Christ could want to do this. Why would a person want to pick up the burden of his sin again and go back to being a slave of Satan! (See John 6:39; 10:28; Rom. 8:35–39; 1 Cor. 1:8–9; Eph. 1:13; 5:27; Phil. 1:6; 2 Tim. 1:12; 4:18; 1 Peter 1:4–5; 1 John 5:12–13; Jude 24–25.)

HEAVEN IS THE SURE DESTINATION OF THE CHRISTIAN AND HIS ETERNAL HOME. If we love someone, we want to be close to them. The born-again child of God wants to spend eternity with God in heaven. The child of God has his name recorded in the "Lamb's book of life" (Rev. 21:27). This is a sure reservation for heaven. (See John 14:1–6; 17:24; 2 Cor. 5:1–2; Phil. 1:23; 3:20–21; Col. 1:5; 1 Thess. 4:17; 2 Tim. 4:18; Heb. 11:16; 1 Peter 1:4–5.)

AFTER A PERSON HAS TRUSTED CHRIST AS HIS OWN PERSONAL SAVIOR AND HAS BECOME A BORN-AGAIN CHILD OF GOD, HE SHOULD:
- Read the Bible daily—Acts 17:11.
- Pray. This is asking things from God, praising Him,

and having fellowship with Him—Luke 18:1.
- Witness for Jesus Christ—Acts 1:8.
- Worship God at a special worship service each week—Hebrews 10:25.

It is possible that the Jehovah's Witness who has agreed to meet with you may be unwilling to answer questions about the Watchtower organization—making inoperative the "groundbreaking approach" which was set forth in Chapter Seven. He may say that he wants only to discuss the Bible. What should you do then?

In the following chapter I explain what to do should this occur.

CHAPTER NINE

WHAT IF THE WITNESS INSISTS ON A BIBLE STUDY?

Although you have informed the Jehovah's Witness with whom you are meeting that you do not have a problem understanding the Bible and want only to inquire about their organization, he will sometimes practically *insist* that you study the Bible with him. If so, you can turn it to your advantage. (Even so, use this approach only if he won't discuss the organization.)

When Jehovah's Witnesses talk about a Bible study, they mean going over the material they have memorized from the Watchtower publications. They never study the Bible independent of their publications. They might tell you that they get their views from just studying the Bible, but this is not true.

Jehovah's Witnesses are not well educated in the Bible. Most Jehovah's Witnesses do not read the Bible individually, so they are not familiar with the context of the verses they use. In fact, I have found that just about every Jehovah's Witness will exaggerate when you ask him how often he has read the entire Bible. Actually, they can't acquire anything firsthand, but take only what the Watchtower publications give them. So when you get Jehovah's Witnesses off their memorized material, they do not know what the Bible teaches.

If the Witness wants to have a Bible study, there are at least four ways in which you can handle this. You will not need to use all the methods I suggest; use only the ones with which you feel most comfortable.

FIRST METHOD

Approach #1: There are several things that we should decide before we begin our Bible study. We don't want to enter into an argument. As you are well aware, there are many false prophets and false religious teachers in the world today. There can be only one true way but many false ways. I really don't know much about you. Shouldn't I know something about where you obtained your teachings before I listen to you? For instance, if I were to let a Mormon into my house and he wanted to teach me, what do you think my reaction ought to be? (They believe the Mormons are false, so will say you should not believe them.) The same is true of the Unification Church, The Way International, The Worldwide Church of God (Armstrongites), etc. None of these groups would come to me and say that they are false prophets. They would claim to speak the truth and tell me all other groups are false. Therefore, I would like to understand more about your organization first, so that I know who has taught you and where you are heading.

Approach #2 (If approach #1 does not work): Is this going to be a Bible study where you intend to be the teacher and I am the student? (If they answer "Yes," continue by saying:) If you intend to be the teacher, I would like to know what qualifications you have for being a Bible teacher. (Then ask these questions:)

Question #1: Are the things you want to teach me conclusions that you came to by reading the Bible without any outside helps? (The answer will be "No," but they might be a little evasive.)

Question #2: Since you did not teach yourself the Bible, then what is your primary source of Bible knowledge? (If they are honest they will have to say they learned it from Watchtower publications.)

Question #3: Since what you want to teach me is secondhand—what comes from the Society and not from your own personal study—then what assurance do I have that your teaching will be accurate?

Question #4: How many times have you read the Bible all the way through?

Question #5: Have you personally read Bible commentaries and books other than the Watchtower publication on the subject you want to teach? (They are very good at deceiving, so it is hard to tell what they might answer. If they answer "Yes," then continue by asking:)

Question #6: Would you please name some Bible commentaries and other books you have read? Are these personal books in your possession? (If "No":) Where did you get these books that you read? (I doubt that you will find many who have done any independent reading, since that is forbidden by the Watchtower. If they claim they have, then you can ask them if they would mind reading a book that you have about the Bible and commenting on it. I am almost 100% sure they will decline.)

Question #7: I understand that there are many quotes, from a variety of sources, to be found in Watchtower publications. Have you ever personally gone to a library and checked out these quotes, reading them in their context, to make sure they are used accurately? (You undoubtedly will not receive an affirmative answer to this question. But if they should say "Yes," then ask them how many quotes they have checked out and at what library, so that if you wish to check them out you will know where to go.)

Question #8: I would like to know if the things you want to teach are the same as what has been taught from the very beginning of your organization? In other words, have there ever been any changes? (If they are truthful, they must admit that there have been many changes.)

Question #9: Would you mind telling me some of the interpretations of Scripture that the Watchtower has felt necessary to change? (Just let them name the changes. Don't try to argue with them about them.)

Question #10: If your interpretations had really been from God in the first place, then there would never have been any need to make changes! Right? How did these incorrect interpretations get into your organization? (At this point, there might be a good possibility of getting them into a discussion of the Watchtower organization, which is what you want to do. You can keep going in this vein by asking more of the questions found in Chapter Seven.)

Question #11: I would imagine that you have access to an extensive library of Watchtower publications. Have you ever gone back and read any of the older publications? If so, were you just looking up certain quotes or did you read some of the books completely? (All Kingdom Halls have a library of old Watchtower publications, but very seldom do Jehovah's Witnesses look at them. They are discouraged from doing so, because if they did they would soon discover the many changes and contradictions. In fact, they are not able to go into the library in the Kingdom Hall and read old Watchtower publications without obtaining permission and having one of the elders with them.)

Question #12: During our study, there might be the possibility of some questions arising concerning what was written in previous Watchtower publications. In that case, would it be possible for you to bring the book from the Kingdom Hall library so that we can both read the quote in context?

Response #1: They don't allow us to take any of the books out of the library. (Here you might ask him if it would be okay for the two of you to go to the Kingdom Hall and look up the quotes under discussion.)

Response #2: I am sure that there have never been any changes, so there shouldn't be the need of looking up any of these references. (Point out if he is so sure, then he should be all the more happy to look at the old publications to reassure *you*.)

Question #13: If you don't want to look up the old Watchtower publications yourself, I do. Would if be okay, if I found any of these publications, that I bring them to our study so we could look at them together? (I have a large library of old Watchtower publications, so I could supply you with a copy of any of the pages you want. See Appendix III about ordering this material.)

Question #14: Usually a qualification for being a good Bible teacher is to have a working knowledge of Greek and Hebrew. I don't think you qualify to be a Greek and Hebrew scholar. Therefore, would you please name me a few of the recognized scholars in Greek and Hebrew among the Jehovah's Witnesses? (We find no recognized Greek and Hebrew scholars among them.)

Response #1: We do not give out the names of our scholars because we do not want them to be praised. We want Jehovah to receive the glory. (This is a polite way of saying they don't have any Greek or Hebrew scholars.)

Response #2: None. (If they are truthful.)

I think by this time you will have taken most of the wind from their sails. Yet if these questions have not fazed them, there are still a few more things you can do.

SECOND METHOD

Once I met two Jehovah's Witnesses on the street and invited them to my house. They came. I mentioned to them that I had questions about the Watchtower Society that I would like to discuss with them, but one insisted that we just use the Bible. He went on for half an hour in this vein. Finally I said, "Okay, we will use the Bible. Wait until I go and get mine." I gathered up about eight different Bibles I had and placed them on the table before him. I then asked him which one of the Bibles he wanted me to use. He said it didn't matter to him which Bible I used. The conversation then went something like this:

Me: Where in the Bible does it say that we need some human person to teach us to understand the Bible?

J.W.: Acts 8:31—where it says, "He said: 'Really, how could I ever do so, unless someone guided me?'" (NWT).

Me: Would it be okay if we look at this in its context?

J.W.: Sure.

Me: Let's start with Acts 8:26, where the story begins, and read to verse 40. (Their Bible reads about the same.) Verse 26 reads, "And the angel of the Lord spake unto Philip, saying, Arise, and go toward the south unto the way that goeth down from Jerusalem unto Gaza, which is desert." This is interesting. We note that an angel spoke to Philip and gave him clear instructions. Do you believe that today angels come down and speak to the men on the governing body and give them clear instructions like we find here?

J.W.: I don't know if I can answer that or not. (The Watchtower Society teaches that angels listen to the councils of heaven and then bring down this information to the men on the governing body. However, it is very hard for a Jehovah's Witness to acknowledge this fact because there are so many mistakes and errors in what the Watchtower leaders have put forth. Because of this, a Jehovah's Witness can't give a straight answer.)

Me: Verse 29 says, "Then the Spirit said unto Philip, Go near, and join thyself to this chariot." This is a very strange verse. The Bible says that "the Spirit spoke" and gave explicit instructions. I thought that Jehovah's Witnesses believe and teach that the Holy Spirit is not a person but just God's "active force"—that is, an inanimate something. How could something that does not have life speak?

J.W.: It probably means the angel mentioned in verse 26.

Me: But it doesn't say "angel" but "the Spirit." I would like for you to explain how an impersonal spirit can speak?

J.W.: I don't think I can answer that for you.

Me: I think you teach that the men on the governing body are among "the anointed" and possess the spirit of God. If this true, does the spirit of God—God's active force—relay information directly to the men on the governing body now?

J.W.: I don't really know. (Have you noticed the doubts I am putting in the minds of the Jehovah's Witnesses as I question them?)

Me: In verses 32 and 33 the Ethiopian eunuch was reading the Bible when Philip met him. When you contact people, do you encourage them to read the Bible and then ask you questions from what they have read in the Bible?

J.W.: Since a person can't really understand the Bible on his own, we encourage people to read Watchtower publications that explain the Bible.

Me: Have you comprehended what is written in verse 35? "Then Philip opened his mouth, and began at the same scripture, and preached unto him Jesus." (The NWT reads, "Philip opened his mouth and, starting with this Scripture, he declared to him the good news about Jesus.") Is this what you do as a Jehovah's Witness when you start talking to people? Do you put the emphasis on Jesus and tell them the good news that Jesus Christ died and shed His precious blood for all their ungodly sins?

J.W.: Well, a . . . (I didn't get much of an answer.)

Me: Verse 39 is really strange in the light of the Watchtower's teachings. The New World Translation says, "When they had come up out of the water, Jehovah's spirit quickly led Philip away, and the eunuch did not see him any more, for he kept going on his way rejoicing." I think the Watchtower Society teaches that a person must be taught by a Jehovah's Witness, using Watchtower publications, from the very beginning *and* that they must *continue* to read them. In this case, the eunuch only had the Bible, which had prepared his heart in the first place. How do you explain this verse in the light of the Watchtower's teachings?

J.W.: (I didn't receive any answer. He closed his Bible at this stage and was glad to go on to something else.)

When you find yourself in a situation where they use a Bible verse, you never want to counter by using another verse. Jehovah's Witnesses take just about every verse they use, or even part of a verse, out of context. If you begin reading the verse in context (like I have illustrated above) and asking them questions about what is written before and after what they have used, you can easily show that the verse doesn't mean what the Watchtower Society says. A few times like this and they will forget about wanting to teach you the Bible. Then you can get on to questions about the organization.

THIRD METHOD

Often the Jehovah's Witness who has come to your house will ask you what subject you would like to study. Generally Christians will suggest the Trinity or the deity of Christ—which makes the Jehovah's Witness happy, because he is well prepared to discuss these subjects. You can tell the Witness that you would like to start where the Bible starts, and that is with *sin*. (In order for a person to have a proper understanding of the Bible he must have a clear idea of sin.) You can turn to the previous chapter and go through all the material I have presented on how to lead a person to Christ. Ask him to read each verse and give you an explanation. He will not be familiar with this material. Since the Watchtower Society doesn't emphasize sin, they have not changed these verses in their Bible. Remember, your purpose is to get him to think. This is an excellent opportunity to clearly explain the whole plan of salvation.

FOURTH METHOD

Explain to him how important it is to read the Bible in context. Thus, if you are going to study the Bible with him, the best way would be to take one book of the New Testament and go through it verse by verse. (You do not have to be a Bible scholar to do this. You just need to ask questions. You can let him think he is the teacher.) The only book the Watchtower Society publishes which studies the Bible in a verse-by-verse manner is one on the Book of Revelation. (This book is usually only for Jehovah's Witnesses to study, and not something they use when they want to teach new people.) They do not know how to conduct a book-by-book, verse-by-verse Bible study. (Do not try to find a Bible-study book to use with them. You can study one beforehand, but they won't study it with you.)

Let's say we start with the book of Ephesians. Here are some examples of questions you can ask them. (Be sure to *ask* them and not *tell* them. But there will be many verses that they can't explain. In these cases, you can suggest an answer and ask them what they think. As I said before, the seed you sow in your question is more important than the content of their answer.)

V. 1: Paul was not one of the original apostles and met Christ only after His death, so why would Paul identify himself as an "apostle of Jesus Christ" and not as an "apostle of Jehovah"?

Why does Paul call these Christians in Ephesus "saints"?

Why does he challenge them to be "faithful in Christ Jesus" and not "faithful to Jehovah"?

What does it mean to be "in Christ"?

How does one come to be considered by God to be "in Christ"?

V. 2: What is this "grace" being shown to the believer? What is this "peace"?

Why are these two important blessings linked as coming from the Father and the Lord Jesus Christ equally?

V. 3: What are these "spiritual blessings in heavenly places"?

What does it mean to be "in Christ" to receive these blessings? It seems like there needs to be some special connection with Christ that is separate from the Father!

V. 4: What does it mean to be "chosen in Christ before the foundation of the world"?

Again we note this expression "in Christ." This seems very important. What do you think?

What special relationship do you have with the Lord Jesus Christ? Can you say that you are "in Christ"?

There seems to be a connection between being "holy and without blame" and being "in Christ." How does the Lord Jesus Christ *make* us holy?

This verse seems to show that we become holy and blameless because of our being "in Christ" and not because of an organizational affiliation or through our own efforts. Would you comment.

Do you have complete assurance that you can stand "holy and blameless" before God? (I trust you see how you can present the claims of Christ through your questions.)

V. 5: "In love" of verse 4 really is the beginning of verse 5. What does it mean to be "predestinated"? Then what does it mean "in love having been predestinated"?

What does it mean to be adopted into the family of God?

Why does it say that this adoption takes place "by Jesus Christ"?

When and how does this adoption take place?

What "good pleasure" does it give God for me to be adopted as one of His children?

V. 6: Who is the "beloved"?

What does it mean to be "accepted in the beloved"?

How do we get to where we are "accepted in the beloved"?

V. 7: Why could Paul say to the Ephesian Christians, "we have redemption"?

What kind of transaction took place to give them such assurance?

Is it possible for people right now to say "we have redemption"?

Please explain how this redemption comes through the blood of the Lord Jesus Christ.

In what way is it possible to know that our personal sins have been forgiven through the blood of the Lord Jesus Christ?

Why does it say that our forgiveness of sins comes through "the riches of his grace" and not through our good works and endurance?

This is just a sample of what can be done. There are many important questions that you can ask. If you studied the Bible with a Jehovah's Witness in this way, it wouldn't be long until he would realize that the Watchtower teachings are not according to the Bible. Also, he should see there is a richness in Christ which he does not possess.

It is wonderful when you are able to get a Jehovah's Witness to realize that the Watchtower Society is not God's channel of communication to this earth. This often opens the door to explain the true way of salvation through the Lord Jesus Christ. However, when a person comes out of the Watchtower and into Christ there are still some important steps that remain. These will be presented in the next chapter.

CHAPTER TEN

THE FINAL STEP

If you have been able to discuss these matters with a Jehovah's Witness, you will have caused him to question the Watchtower organization and will have had the opportunity also to present the true gospel of Jesus Christ. But even when a Jehovah's Witness recognizes that the Watchtower organization is not "the truth," it is not a simple thing for him just to walk away. The Watchtower Society has made it as difficult as possible for anyone to leave the organization—by means of their disfellowshipping policy. There is no way that a Jehovah's Witness can come out of the cult and still stay in the good graces of the organization and its followers. Whether they disfellowship him or he asks to be dissociated, the end result is the same: they will spread lies about the person, and no Jehovah's Witness will have anything more to do with him.

Since a Jehovah's Witness ordinarily associates only with other Jehovah's Witnesses, this leaves him without anyone to have fellowship with if he leaves the organization. He is completely isolated. This is one of the worst things that can happen to any person in this life. Humans can get by with very little material wealth, but to be without friends is a very difficult thing to cope with.

Though the Jehovah's Witnesses do not believe in a hell in the hereafter, they have created a hell here on earth for anyone who dares to leave their organization. For married individuals, it often means the loss of his or her mate. If one's parents, children, or grandchildren are in the organization, the person will lose them also. Thus there is a tremendous struggle as a Jehovah's Witness realizes that the Watchtower is not God's organization. He must choose to leave a false system, on the one hand, or to leave all his associates and perhaps even his family on the other. A Christian needs to appreciate the difficult decision the Jehovah's Witness has to make.

I have heard of many cases where, though a Jehovah's Witness knows that the Watchtower system is false, he will deliberately stay in for a while. Once disfellowshipped, he cannot speak to any of his Jehovah's Witness associates or family, for they will not associate with him. Before this happens, he will attempt to help the others to come to the same conclusion that the Watchtower is false. A number have been successful at this. Of course, one can only get by with it for a year or so before being disfellowshipped, but he has used the opportunity he had. So when someone you have been witnessing to doesn't come out immediately upon acknowledging that the Watchtower is a false religion, be very patient and do not condemn him. Let him know you are still there and willing to help. He might be able to reach some other Jehovah's Witnesses—ones an outsider can't.

Once a person leaves the Kingdom Hall, he rarely starts attending church right away. He will generally go into a period of limbo. Once he realizes that the Watchtower Society has badly deceived him, it will take time before he can trust anyone else. You need to show him a lot of love, patience and understanding. Do *not* rush him. If he feels reluctant, do not urge him to start attending church immediately. He has been taught that Satan will enter his heart if he goes into a church. So, along with not being able to trust anyone, there is still this awful fear remaining in him.

It might be best to begin with a weekly Bible study in your home. Study books such as John, Romans, Galatians or Ephesians. Most of the meanings are clear. Read verse by verse so that he can begin to understand it. Keep it simple, and he will realize that the Bible is not that difficult to understand. He will learn that he can understand the Bible without the Watchtower Society's help. Encourage him to read the

Bible on his own during the week. Be careful about using a Bible study guidebook, because he was deceived by books in the past. Once he begins to understand the Bible and has more confidence in you, invite him to church, but don't pressure him to attend if he still doesn't feel ready.

Besides teaching him the Bible, it is important to listen to him concerning the problems he is having. He will need a lot of support because he will be shunned by family and friends. Be the first one he can talk to.

Be very patient with him when he doesn't discard all the Watchtower doctrines and directives immediately. Most ex-Jehovah's Witnesses are out of the Watchtower organization long before the Watchtower is out of them. Understanding the Trinity, the immortality of the soul, and the doctrine of hell are the most difficult. Upon being saved and into the Bible, he will begin to see these biblical teachings through your patient instruction and the help of the Holy Spirit . . . but it will take time.

Though it is a long and difficult process to lead a Jehovah's Witness out of the Watchtower Society and into new life in Christ, it is often just about as difficult to get him to where he feels comfortable in a church. I know this is true because I spoke to a lady who had come out of the Watchtower who told me of the effort she had to put forth before church members accepted her. Why? Some Christians seem to look upon a former cult member as carrying some kind of plague. It is a very sad thing, but in many of our churches any new person has to be patient and work his way into the church. He is often not welcomed with open arms. Many old-timers in the church have their own close friends. They don't want to let anyone else get close to them, nor do they care to go to the effort of making new friends. For this reason, you need to do all you possibly can to get the church ready to welcome this ex-Jehovah's Witness.

There are several ways this can be done. If the church is faithfully praying for you while you are dealing with the Jehovah's Witness, they will be familiar with the name and have a greater interest in this person. When you do bring him, try to introduce him to as many people as possible—especially to the ones you know are more apt to welcome a new person and recall his name. Also, remember that the second week is more important than the first week. He will expect to be noticed the first week, but if he comes back the next week and people not only recall that he attended the week before but remember his name, it will make a real impression upon him.

Of course, the church needs to *continue* working at making him feel welcome. You definitely need to alert them not to try to set him straight on all the Watchtower doctrines the first time he attends. This could set him back months or maybe years! Let him know that he is welcome just the way he is. It takes the average person some time to get his theology correct, let alone a Jehovah's Witness. Any sort of pressure may backfire. If it is a gospel-preaching church, and he feels comfortable there, he will gradually come to understand the major biblical doctrines and precepts.

A Jehovah's Witness has a real problem with seeing a cross. He has been brainwashed into thinking that Christians worship the cross and so he has come to hate it. When an ex-Jehovah's Witness comes into a church that has a cross in the front of the sanctuary, and especially a large one, he will often cringe and want to leave. If you have a cross in your church, it is best to tell him before he enters the building. Explain that Bible-believing Christians do not worship the cross: it is there to remind us of the awful death that Jesus Christ endured to bring salvation to us sinners. By letting him know that there is a cross and explaining the meaning, it should make it a little easier for him to enter and remain in the church.

Leading a Jehovah's Witnesses out of the Watchtower Society and into Christ is not easy, but it will be one of the most rewarding experiences of your Christian life. Remember the words of James 5:20: "Let him know, that he which converteth the sinner from the error of his way shall save a soul from death, and shall hide a multitude of sins."

One thing even a brainwashed Jehovah's Witnesses can't resist is the pressure of encountering many Christians who *know how to witness successfully*. If enough Christians would begin to use the material found in this book, I am confident that the growth of the Watchtower Society could be stopped and many who believe in it would be saved. I have placed the tools in your hands so that you can be a more effective witness to Jehovah's Witnesses.

We all have to start somewhere. My prayer is that you will use every opportunity you have to witness to these needy, lost souls.

APPENDIX I

HOW TO USE WATCHTOWER LITERATURE EFFECTIVELY IN WITNESSING

I have found that using Watchtower literature in witnessing to Jehovah's Witnesses can be very effective.

Jehovah's Witnesses have been taught very early in their indoctrination process that any kind of opposition is from the devil. Thus when you try to point out the false doctrines and unveil the many errors and changes in the Watchtower teachings, they will regard you as an emissary of Satan and resist you. It is, therefore, difficult to speak to a Jehovah's Witness realistically about this situation. Mostly it ends in an argument and merely convinces the Jehovah's Witness all the more that he is right because of the opposition he is receiving. This is especially difficult if the one you are trying to witness to is a family member or close friend. If you are looking for a more effective way, this chapter will be of particular interest to you.

Do not fight their use of their literature but use it to your advantage. Just as a Christian wants a Jehovah's Witness to read sound Christian literature, so the Jehovah's Witness wants the Christian to read his literature. When you receive his literature and promise to read it, you can open his heart instead of closing it. (If you happen to be married to a Jehovah's Witness, he or she will have an abundance of literature lying around for you to pick up and read.)

You can truthfully say to the Witness, "I would really like to understand your religion. [Note: You did *not* say "believe."] I will read your literature, but I am sure I will have many questions. Since you have studied what the Watchtower Society teaches, would you be willing to answer my questions? That would enable me to understand the Watchtower's teachings better."

You will generally receive an affirmative and enthusiastic answer, since Jehovah's Witnesses are instructed that they are the ones to teach and not to be taught. They will be elated that they can teach! As you read their literature, you can ask many of the doubt-sowing questions I have listed below. Also, you can use the questions found in Chapter Seven.

When a Jehovah's Witness conducts a so-called "home Bible study" with a person, he generally wants to use the Watchtower publication *You Can Live Forever in Paradise on Earth*. The organization wrote this especially for this purpose. It gives an overview of the Watchtower's basic teachings. (I have studied this book with a Jehovah's Witness elder and had a tremendous opportunity to ask questions that caused him to think. I also presented the gospel through my questions in an indirect way.) The best thing about using their material is they can't get upset with you! Since you are willing to use their book and ask questions from what you have read, it obligates them to cooperate with you in trying to understand their religion. Thus you throw the burden on them to prove that the Watchtower Society has the truth. (This, of course, is impossible for them to do.)

Remember that the Watchtower authors write their publications to be accepted. And for an unquestioning mind, they can be beguiling. But a Jehovah's Witness is not supposed to ask any questions even though the writings may be illogical. They are simply supposed to accept the teachings. It is very difficult for them to explain most of what is written in their publications. You will find that they do not have an answer for most of the questions that I am about to give you to ask. In this way, the one with whom you are conversing will begin to realize that the Watchtower Society really does not have the answers for many problems. And if you should happen to be in possession of old Watchtower literature that contains their false prophecies or other outdated teachings, you will have a very good opportunity to present this material—and there will be an excellent chance of their looking at it.

The following questions are ones that I have thought up as I read the 1989 Watchtower publication *You Can Live Forever in Paradise on Earth*. Once you understand what kind of questions to look for, you can create your own questions.

Chapter 1
LIVING FOREVER NOT JUST A DREAM

They base this chapter on the false assumption that God created this earth for everyone to live upon forever, without ever going to heaven or hell. They describe some of the present horrible conditions on this earth and then hold out the hope of a beautifully restored earth. They do not start by offering a solution to the sin problem that separates humanity from God and has caused these awful conditions. Instead, they appeal to the selfish desires of our human flesh by offering their idea of what the earth will be like during the Millennium. Of course, they do not inform the reader that if their ideas are true, Jehovah's Witnesses must spend one thousand years of hard labor building and maintaining it.

• On pages 12 and 13 there is a beautiful fall scene showing miles of sprawling acreage. A lake is in the middle of the picture, with a snowcapped mountain in the background. In the foreground there are nine happy-looking people. Some of them are picking and packing apples. There is one average-size house in the middle of the picture.

Question #1: To me this is not a realistic picture. Where are the roads? Where are the factories that will be needed to make the furniture for the houses, clothes for the people, and material to build houses, etc.? Where are the stores? I don't see any machinery to cut the large wheat field. Surely that can't be done by hand!

Question #2: If I understand the Watchtower's approach, they put forth the best possible living conditions a person could dream of in the pictures in their publications.

However, in reality the living conditions are likely not to be that ideal. Would I be correct in coming to such a conclusion?

• On page 14, paragraph 15, line 9, it says, "But those who are serving God will survive the end." They teach that this world will be almost destroyed at Armageddon and after this the Jehovah's Witnesses must rebuild this earth.

Question #1: Would you please explain what is going to happen when this world ends?

Question #2: How will it be possible for only Jehovah's Witnesses to escape being killed?

Question #3: How will the Jehovah's Witnesses go about getting this destroyed earth back to the condition that is presented in your pictures? (At this point, you can go through the list of questions I presented in Chapter Seven under the heading "Building the New Earth.")

Chapter 2
AN ENEMY OF EVERLASTING LIFE

This chapter has to do with Satan and places the blame for the evil in this world upon him. They say Satan controls the people of this earth through false religion. They further state that Satan was cast out of heaven in 1914 and is now living upon this earth, causing all the evil. They claim that the end of Satan's rule will come shortly.

• In this chapter we are informed that Satan is "an intelligent unseen person" (page 16), yet is "a real person" (page 18), and "very powerful" (page 20).

Question #1: If I understand the Watchtower's teachings correctly, Jesus Christ did not have any superior power in Himself when He was on this earth. His mighty power and knowledge came through "God's active force." Also I believe the Watchtower teaches that the Father created the Son and then the Son created everything else. Thus Satan would have to have been created by the Son and would obviously be lower than the Son. Yet the Son could only act as He received power from God through His active force. In light of this, I would like to know where Satan gets his power?

Question #2: Here is a real mystery to me. The Watchtower teaches that the force for evil, Satan, is "an intelligent spirit," "a real person," and "very powerful." However, the Watchtower teaches that the force for good, the Holy Spirit, is not a real person and does not possess intelligence. I can't see how they can deny the personality of the Holy Spirit and make Him some indescribable "active force," and all the while claim that Satan, whom they cannot see either, is intelligent and a real person. Could you please explain this mystery to me?

• On page 22, paragraph 18, line 1, it says, "When did this war in heaven take place? The evidence shows that it happened around the time of World War I, which began in 1914."

Question #1: It seems to me that I heard that the Watchtower first taught that Christ began to reign invisibly in 1874 and it was then that Christ cast Satan out of heaven. How did they make such a mistake?

Question #2: If they arrived at the 1874 date by studying the Bible, then someone miscalculated! Who made this mistake?

Question #3: If they came to the 1914 date by the same reasoning as for the 1874 date—that being based on certain outward signs—then how do we know that the signs for the 1914 calculation were not as misleading as those authenticating the 1874 date were?

Question #4: If I remember correctly, until 1930 the Watchtower taught that Christ had returned invisibly in 1874. If there were so many signs that Satan was thrown out of heaven and Christ began His reign in 1914, as this book states, then why, for those sixteen years prior to 1930, was there no clear evidence of this?

• On page 23, paragraph 22, line 1, it states, "If we are to receive everlasting life, we need accurate knowledge about God, his King-Son and his kingdom. (John 17:3)"

Question #1: This is a confusing statement. As I read the Bible, it continually speaks about "faith." Where is the balance between this "taking in knowledge" and having faith?

Let me explain the reason for my being perplexed. I believe that Jesus Christ existed before He came into this world. (Don't enter a discussion on the deity of Christ at this point.) I further believe that two thousand years ago He was born into this world through the virgin Mary. He lived a sinless, perfect life. In the end He was tortured and died in agony (Don't use the word "cross"). I believe that He shed His blood for all my personal sins. I came to realize that my heart was full of sins like pride, self-centeredness, selfishness, anger, wrath, lying, cheating, gossip, jealousy, covetousness, unthankfulness, backbiting, evil thoughts, lust, etc. I then confessed my sins to God and in faith believed that Jesus Christ had died for all my personal sins. Since Christ has died for all my sins, then all of them are washed away in His blood and I received eternal life the moment I trusted in what Christ did for me. Because I was saved through faith, I can't grasp the connection between what the Bible calls "faith" and what the Watchtower calls "taking in knowledge." Could you explain this to me?

(I was able to present the plan of salvation in my question without any resistance. When I used this question, after he had sat for a little while thinking of what I had said, my Jehovah's Witness friend's reply was, "I have really never thought of it that way.")

• On page 23 it mentions about "examining the Scriptures" and on page 24 about "studying the Bible."

Question #1: When you started studying with the Witnesses did they encourage you to read the Bible independent of the Watchtower publications—so that you could become familiar with the Bible and examine the context of the verses they quoted, to make sure the interpretation they had put on various verses was accurate?

Question #2: While studying with the Witnesses, have

you spent more time reading the Bible or reading the Watchtower publications?

• In several places on pages 23 and 24 it mentions that a person might receive opposition when he starts studying with the Jehovah's Witnesses. They believe that this opposition is from Satan and should be resisted.

Question #1: The Bible warns that in the last days there will be many false prophets and religions. I think the Mormons, Moonies, The Worldwide Church of God, Jehovah's Witnesses, etc., could all be considered as religious groups coming forth in the latter days. The Bible clearly says that we are not to believe every religious group that comes along . . . certainly not just because they say they are right (see 1 John 4:1–3). If I remember correctly, the Bible says that we should "inquire, make search, and ask diligently" about all religions (see Deut. 13:14). Why does the Bible warn us that we should take great caution when it comes to religions that have developed in recent years, and yet the Watchtower Society tells you that you should *resist* all warnings as coming from Satan?

Question #2: Let us suppose that the Mormons had come to your door before the Jehovah's Witnesses did. If relatives or friends found out about it and warned you about them, wouldn't you consider that they had done you a great favor if they kept you out of that false religion?

Question #3: I don't understand why opposition or warnings from friends should automatically be considered as from the devil and hence make the Watchtower the true religion. Catholics who become Protestants receive opposition. Muslims who become Christians receive opposition. Just about everyone who changes his religious affiliation receives opposition. Why would receiving some warnings necessarily be of the devil?

Question #4: I would like to know what could be wrong with thoroughly checking out a religious group? We have to realize that there are many false groups, but only one true one. The possibility of joining a false group is much higher than that of joining the right one. Correct? I think that people should appreciate all the warnings, help and advice they might receive when they are looking into a religion! In many situations we become so emotionally involved that we cannot see all the ramifications. Instead of automatically considering all warnings to be of the devil, might they not best be regarded as loving concern for another person? Maybe those persons know something about the Watchtower way that has not been presented to you—something that might be very helpful to you in making your decision?

Question #5: Since some religious groups are easy to get into but very hard to get out of, wouldn't it be best for a person to spend time investigating the group he is interested in and getting all the advice he can from other people before he joins?

Chapter 3
YOUR RELIGION REALLY MATTERS

This chapter urges people to investigate their religion in the light of the Bible. It states that there can be only one true way and makes the claim that the Watchtower is that way. But Jehovah's Witnesses are not willing to take their own advice. It is fine to challenge other people to investigate their religion, but they are unwilling to investigate theirs. They will not even examine their own literature of a few years ago.

• On pages 32 and 33 people are asked, if proof were given to them that they belong to the wrong religion, would they leave that religion and join the true one. Yet there are many Jehovah's Witnesses who know the Watchtower way is not correct but they are not willing to leave.

Question #1: I find this chapter interesting. If I understand correctly what is written here, Jehovah's Witnesses strongly urge inquirers to spend much time in reading the Bible independent of the Watchtower publications so that when they come across verses used in the publications they will immediately know if they are used in context and in harmony with the rest of the Bible. Would this conclusion be correct? (In light of what the Society writes, it will be hard for them to answer in the affirmative but also hard to answer in the negative. Listen closely to their answer, because they probably will use double-talk.)

Question #2: Since the Watchtower urges people of other religious affiliations to investigate *their* religions, then you surely will not mind if I investigate the Watchtower organization in the same way, will you?

Question #3: On page 31, paragraph 15, line 1, it says, "Since many religions today are not doing God's will, we cannot simply assume that the teachings of the religious organization we are associated with are in agreement with God's Word. The mere fact that the Bible is used by a religion does not of itself prove that all the things it teaches and practices are in the Bible. It is important that we ourselves examine whether they are or not." How did you examine the Watchtower way before you joined? What are some of the books you read on the opposite side while you were reading the Watchtower material?

Chapter 4
GOD—WHO IS HE?

This chapter deals with the existence of God and the kind of person He is. Also, they discuss the deity of Jesus Christ and the Trinity, God's name, and how to worship Jehovah. This is an important chapter because it clearly shows that the God of the Watchtower is not the omnipotent, omnipresent, Triune God of the Bible.

• On page 36, paragraph 6, line 7, it says, "Although he does not have a material body, he has a spiritual one. A spirit person has a body? Yes, the Bible says: 'If there is a physical body, there is also a spiritual one.'—1 Corinthians 15:44; John 4:24."

Question #1: I have never heard before about spirit beings, including God, having spirit bodies. I do not have the faintest idea why they would need one or what it is like. Would you be so kind as to describe what a spirit body is like? (I don't think you will receive much of an answer.)

Question #2: To be a "person" one has to have (1) personality, (2) mind, and (3) a will. Is the person's essence contained in the spirit or is it found in the spirit body? (This will be an entirely new thought to them, so it is hard to tell what their reply will be; but I am sure they will not be able to explain their doctrine.)

Question #3: I read John 4:24 but it does not say that God has a spirit body. It only says that "God is a spirit." I don't know of anyone (except the Mormons) who has a problem with the fact that God is a spirit. I can't understand what connection this verse has with proving that God has a spirit body. Would you please explain what connection this verse has? (It is best to ignore their misuse of 1 Corinthians 15:44 here, for that passage can become a minefield.)

• On page 36, paragraph 7, line 1, it says, "Since God is a person with a spiritual body, he must have a place to live."

Question #1: This seems to me a very dogmatic statement. Would you please tell me where God lives? (You are almost certain to receive the answer, "I don't know.")

Question #2: I have heard that the Watchtower used to teach that God lived in the constellation Pleiades on the star Alcyone. Is this still the teaching of the Watchtower? (If you have copies of their literature proclaiming this fact, do not show it to them at this time. Wait until next week. Most are not familiar with the teaching and will not know how to answer. Some will clearly deny the teaching. If they deny that God still lives there, then continue with the next question.)

Question #3: If I remember correctly, as late as 1928 the Watchtower taught that God lived on the star Alcyone. Since you are so sure that God does not live there anymore, would you tell me where He moved to?

• On page 37, paragraph 9, line 8, it says, "He can send out his spirit, his active force, to do whatever he wants though he is far away."

Question #1: Since the Watchtower confines God to "a spirit body with a place to live" and that place is "far away," it seems to me that He is limited by restrictions. Would you please comment?

Question #2: This point confuses me. If spirit beings have spirit bodies, then angels also would have spirit bodies. We know that angels can travel between heaven and earth. Yet the Watchtower has God staying in just one place. It seems that angels can do something that God Himself cannot do! Don't you think that it is odd for God to give more power to angels than He has Himself?

Question #3: Since the God of the Watchtower is confined to a place in heaven, then what would happen if the angels should ever rebel against God? Would this mean that God would no longer know what was going on upon this earth?

• On page 37, paragraph 9, line 3, it says, "It is similar with God, He is in the heavens. . . . Yet his holy spirit, which is his invisible active force, can be felt everywhere, over all the universe. By his holy spirit God created the heavens, the earth and all living things."

Question #1: Since the Holy Spirit is only "an impersonal force" according to the Watchtower, how can God tell it what to do since it is apparently something not a part of God Himself?

Question #2: How could this impersonal force create the world? How can something that doesn't truly exist create something with existence, especially something as profound as this universe?

• On page 40, paragraph 16, line 10, it says, "So we find that some translations of John 1:1 give the correct idea of the original language when they read: . . . 'a god.'" (Do not get into a discussion on the Trinity but just stick to the following three questions.)

Question #1: I do not understand what the Watchtower is trying to prove by making John 1:1 read "a god." If I understand the Watchtower's teaching correctly, they say that since the definite article in the Greek is not found in front of the second word for God in that verse that it can be rendered "a" god. Six hundred years before John 1:1 was written, Isaiah 9:6 identified Jesus Christ as "Mighty God"— and both "M" and "G" are in capitals in your New World Translation of the Bible. (I know they will be fast in saying He is not called the "almighty God." But that is not the point of this argument.) Notice that Jesus is called "God" with a capital "G." Since Isaiah 9:6 has identified Jesus Christ as "Mighty God," then surely Jesus should not be demoted to just "a" god in John 1:1. Shouldn't John 1:1 be taken in the light of Isaiah 9:6 and be translated to harmonize with it?

Question #2: I see another discrepancy: in John 1:6 the definite article is not found before the word "God" in the Greek. Yet the Society translates "God" here with a capital "G." Why do you think they did this?

Question #3: How do you explain Matthew 1:23 in light of what the Society has written about John 1:1? This verse reads, "Behold, a virgin shall be with child, and shall bring forth a son, and they shall call his name Emmanuel, which being interpreted is, God with us." In the Greek the definite article (*ho*) is before "God." Thus the literal translation reads, "With us the God." Since this verse identifies Jesus Christ as "the God," He could not be just "a god" separate from the Godhead, could He? Please explain this to me? (They probably will use a completely different argument for this verse than they did for John 1:1. They might say that Jesus was just "God's representative." But this is not what the Bible says.)

• On page 43, paragraph 23, line 8, it says, "It is not known exactly how it was pronounced, even though some scholars think 'Yahweh' is correct. However, the form 'Jehovah' has been in use for many centuries and is most widely known."

Question: Every dictionary and encyclopedia that I know of says that "Jehovah" is a false rendering for the name LORD in Hebrew and the most correct rendering is "Yahweh." I do not have any problem using the name "Yahweh," but the Watchtower Society seems to. I do not see how Jehovah's Witnesses can be glorifying His name by using what they admit to be an erroneous rendering! Even if the form "Jehovah" is most widely known, I think it would be best to use the spelling and pronunciation closest to the correct name, "Yahweh," and then teach people this name! What good is it to pass on a false name simply because it has come down through years of tradition? Shouldn't we be more interested in accuracy than in tradition?

• On page 46, paragraph 31, line 1, it says, "Worshiping Jehovah, the Creator, in the way he directs is certain to bring us genuine happiness."

Question #1: They have titled this section: "How to Worship Jehovah." It proceeds to say that we should not use idols in worship. For most groups this is no problem, because they don't use idols. But I can't understand what it means to worship Jehovah. Would you please explain this to me?

Question #2: Many Bible-believing groups have a special worship service each week. They sing songs that exalt God and give praise to Him. The authors wrote these songs to help the worshiper focus his thoughts on eternal truths. Many hymns center their messages on the attributes of God, so that He may be known and worshiped for who He is. Of course, these Bible-believing individuals continue to worship and praise Him daily. Do the Jehovah's Witnesses have a special weekly service for worshiping Yahweh?

Question #3: I draw the conclusion from this section that the primary purpose of worshiping Yahweh is "to bring us genuine happiness." I thought that the purpose for worshiping Yahweh was for His glory and exaltation, and not that we might gain His favor so as to receive His blessings. Will you please explain this to me?

Chapter 5
IS THE BIBLE REALLY FROM GOD?

Generally, what is presented in this chapter about the

Bible is accurate. Though the Watchtower Society claims to believe all the Bible as the inspired Word of God, they do not believe it can be read and understood by the average person. They believe that the Bible must be "illuminated," and this can only be done by the men on the governing body. They present this illumination in the Watchtower publications, so the Jehovah's Witnesses must read these instead of the Bible.

It seems evident that they believe in "thought inspiration" instead of "verbal inspiration." "Thought inspiration" means that God merely gave the ideas to men and then they worked the details out in their own words. "Verbal inspiration" means that God not only guided in the main ideas but also in the choice of the words the human authors used.

• On page 47, paragraph 3, line 7, it says, "Today almost everybody on earth can read the Bible in his own language." (Note: The whole Bible is in 322 languages. Yet the NWT is only in twelve. However, the Watchtower magazine and literature is available in 200 languages. Apparently Watchtower literature is more important than the Bible!)

Question #1: It is really wonderful that the Bible is in so many languages and most of the people in the world can read it. How did the Bible get into these languages? (They must admit that groups that have no affiliation with the Watchtower have translated the Bible into these languages.)

Question #2: How many different languages has the New World Translation been translated into? (They might be a little vague, so you should say that you heard it was only in twelve.)

Question #3: This seems to show that there are many groups besides the Jehovah's Witnesses interested in getting the Bible into the hands of people in their languages so they can understand it. Would you agree with this?

Question #4: Since the Bible is available in so many languages, then why are there not more Jehovah's Witnesses —since the Watchtower claims to be based solely on the Bible? If the Watchtower's beliefs are so plain in the Bible, shouldn't everyone come out with the same conclusions as the Jehovah's Witnesses? (If they come up with the typical argument that authorized people must explain the Bible, you can ask, "In other words, God's Word, the Bible, is not enough. It takes some fallible men to illuminate the Bible?")

Question #5: Since it is so important to have an accurate Bible in the hands of all the people of the world and there are many tribes that still do not have the Bible, does the Watchtower support any group whose main purpose is to translate the Bible where it has never been done before? (If they are honest they must say "No." You can ask them why, since the Bible is so important.)

• On page 49, paragraph 8, line 5, it says, "The secretary writes the letter, but the letter contains the thoughts and ideas of the businessman."

Question: (Make this a thought-provoking question rather than one where you are hunting for a certain answer.) This leads me to conclude that the Watchtower Society believes in "thought inspiration" and not "verbal inspiration." Would I be correct in this assumption?

Chapter 6
JESUS CHRIST—SENT BY GOD?

As can be expected, the doctrines set forth in this chapter are greatly perverted, because the Watchtower refuses to give Jesus Christ the same place the Bible gives Him. While saying they believe in Jesus Christ, they go to great length to dethrone Him from His appropriate position in the Godhead. They make many vague statements but never explain them. They do not come out clearly and present their beliefs, but cover them up in a lot of double-talk.

• On page 57, paragraph 3, line 4, under the section titled "He Had Lived Before," it says, "But how could a woman who had never had sexual relations with a man have a child? It was by means of God's holy spirit. Jehovah transferred the life of his mighty spirit Son from heaven to the womb of the virgin Mary." (This is but one of the many deceptive and double-talk sections found in Watchtower publications.)

Following this, on page 58, paragraph 4, line 1, it says, "So before being born on earth as a man Jesus had been in heaven as a mighty spirit person. He had a spirit body invisible to man, just as God has. (John 4:24)"

Question #1: We talked before about "spirit beings" having "spirit bodies." I still do not see where they find this in the Bible, but I would like to move on to a related question. In the case of spirit beings, would you say that the real self is in the spirit or in the spirit body in which the spirit dwells? (I don't think you will get a clear-cut answer.)

Question #2: Since you can't answer this question, let us go from the known to the unknown and see if that will help. If I understand the Watchtower teaching correctly, man has a body, which is his real self—possessing a mind, will and personality. He also has a "spirit" or "life force," but this is just the breath that keeps his body living. It lacks human qualities. Since the real self is found in the body, would it be safe to say that the same is true with a spirit being—that the real self is actually in the spirit body? (Again, I don't think you will receive an answer, but you are making them think.)

Question #3: Taking the statement "Jehovah transferred the life of his mighty spirit Son from heaven to the womb of the virgin Mary" literally, I come to the conclusion that God's Son, who is a spirit person, came down and dwelt in the human body that Mary gave to Jesus. Thus the one who was born would be both human and divine. Is this correct? (They do not believe that any part of the Son in heaven actually came down to this earth. They teach that Jesus was only a man when He lived upon earth. Listen very carefully to how your "teacher" answers you. They *really* teach that at the time of Jesus' conception in the womb of Mary, the Son willed Himself out of existence. They use the words of Philippians 2:7 where it says, "But [he] made himself of no reputation" as a proof text for this belief. I don't know how anyone can get such a meaning out of this verse, but the Watchtower's leaders are good at stretching and twisting the meaning of verses.)

Question #4: If Jesus was *not* both divine and human, then what does the book mean by this statement: "Jehovah transferred the life of his mighty spirit Son from heaven to the womb of the virgin Mary?" What was this "life" that was transferred? (They probably will say that it was just the "life force" that came down.)

Question #5: Since the "life force" is only the breath of man, without any human qualities, then when the Society says the life force came down, they are really saying that nothing personal came down. Wouldn't this be correct?

Question #6: Since spirit beings do not have physical bodies, then they do not have lungs and the need to breathe, do they? So they evidently have no life force. Or do they have lungs of some kind? If so, what do spirit bodies breathe?

Question #7: Since nothing of the Son's "spirit body" came down and dwelt in the human body of Jesus, was the Son still existing in heaven? (At this point they probably will tell you that He willed Himself out of existence.)

Question #8: I have never heard of a spirit being ceasing to exist. Could you please explain to me how this happened? (No answer.)

Question #9: If it is true that the Son willed Himself out of existence, then there are only two possible ways I can think of how this could happen: (1) God would have had to kill Him. But this would be impossible because the Bible says, "the wages of *sin* is death" (Rom. 6:23). Since the Son was perfect and had never sinned, then the Father could not be just and kill His Son. (2) The Son would have had to kill Himself by committing suicide. I have never read about any spirit being ever going out of existence, so I don't have any idea of how He could have committed suicide. Besides, I thought that the Bible teaches that suicide is a sin. Will you please solve this problem for me?

Question #10: This is all very confusing to me and sounds like a great mystery. But I have another question concerning this. If the Son committed suicide, then there would not be any life in existence to transfer to this earth. Please help me to understand this.

Question #11:   Would you say that I am correct in coming to the conclusion that nothing really came down from heaven and Jesus was just a mortal man?

• On page 60, paragraph 11, line 1, it says, "How important to Jesus was this work of making known his Father's name and kingdom?" (Note: Jesus referred to the Father about 350 times. However, He used the name "Yahweh" very sparingly. In the NWT there are only twenty places recorded where Jesus used the word "Yahweh." Most of these were in quotations from the Hebrew Scriptures—the Old Testament. By contrast, Jesus used the word "God" over 180 times and "Father" roughly 175 times. Never did Jesus address the Father as "Yahweh," nor did He ever tell His followers to address the Father as "Yahweh." By his example in Matthew 6:9, Jesus taught that we should address God as "Father.")

Question: Jesus never addressed the Father by the name "Yahweh." Since Jesus did not use the name "Yahweh" for "making known his Father's name," then how can the Watchtower make such a statement?

• On page 62, paragraph 17, line 1, it says, "Jesus died at 33 1/2 years of age. But on the third day after his death he was resurrected to life. Forty days later he returned to heaven. There, as a spirit person once more, he appeared 'before the person of God for us,' carrying the value of his ransom sacrifice." On page 66, paragraph 25, line 1 it says, "There are three parts to the life of God's son. First, there are the unknown number of years he spent with his Father in heaven before he became a human. Next, the 33 1/2 years he spent on earth after his birth. And now there is his life back in heaven as a spirit person."

Question #1: Because this section is so confusing, I read the next two chapters which are about the spirit and soul to see if they might clarify the subject. This did not help me but only confused the situation. As we talked before, we came to the conclusion that the Son willed Himself out of existence at the time Jesus was born on this earth. Then why does it say that the Son spent 33 1/2 years on earth? This would be impossible because He didn't exist. Please explain.

Question #2: If I read this book correctly and understand the Watchtower's teaching, man is made up of a human body and a spirit—which is the breath in man that keeps him alive. This is also known as the "life force." The body of Jesus, the real self, went into the grave, never to be seen again. The spirit of Jesus never died because it is not something that has life and therefore cannot die. On page 77 it states that the spirit no longer exists when the human body dies. Therefore, there was nothing in Jesus that could be resurrected. The word "resurrection" means that the same thing that fell down stood up again. I would like to know how the Watchtower can talk of a resurrection when, according to Watchtower doctrine, after the human dies his body goes to the grave or returns to gasses and is not resurrected. Exactly what was raised?

Question #3: I read earlier on page 31, "The religion that is approved by God must agree in every way with the Bible." But while the Watchtower prints such a statement, they themselves teach things that disagree with the clear teaching of Scripture. One such passage where we can see such a contradiction is Luke 24:36–39. Here we read about an appearance of Jesus Christ after His death and resurrection. According to verse 37, the disciples were not yet fully convinced of the bodily resurrection of Jesus Christ and they thought maybe they had seen "a spirit." Which is what the Watchtower teaches. However, in this very same passage, Jesus clearly says that He was *not* "a spirit person." He said that a spirit person does not have "flesh and bones." Since the Bible clearly says that the resurrected Jesus was not "a spirit," then on what grounds can the Watchtower made such a statement?

Question #4: On page 73 of this book I read that the

"himself" is the actual body, which, of course, the Watchtower claims is the real self. In Luke 24:39 Jesus identifies Himself by saying, "It is I myself." The "myself" could be none other than the body of Jesus. If the body of Jesus was in the grave, then this personage standing before the disciples should not have said "It is I myself," but He does. Again I ask, why does the Watchtower teach something that is the opposite of what the Bible says?

• On page 66, paragraph 26, line 1, it says, "Clearly, Jesus was to become a king."

Question #1: Jesus is the earthly name given to this perfect man. Never in prophecy do we read of this name being used. The Bible never called the Son "Jesus" in the preexistent world. Since the Watchtower teaches that the earthly Jesus died and went into the grave, never to be seen again, how can they say "Jesus was to become a king?" How could someone who died and never has risen from the dead become a king? Since the Watchtower theologians really believe that it is the exalted Michael (and not Jesus at all) who will reign as king, why don't they just call him Michael instead of using the name of a dead man?

Question #2: As we have seen, it is Michael who will reign for a thousand years, according to the Watchtower Society. I would like to know what Michael did to be exalted from "a god" (John 1:1, NWT) to the "Mighty God" (Isaiah 9:6)? I can't understand why Michael should deserve such a promotion when the only thing he did was to commit suicide so Jesus could be born and live on this earth for 33 1/2 years!

• On page 68, paragraph 26, line 2, it says, "He will rule as king . . . forever, and there will be no end of his kingdom." (Note: The Watchtower really teaches that Christ will only reign for 1000 years. They use 1 Corinthians 15:24 and say that after the 1000 years Christ will turn over the kingdom to the Father and *He* will take over. Christ will be demoted from "Mighty God" to "a god" again.)

Question #1: Am I to take this statement literally? If so, am I to understand that Christ will reign for 1000 years over this earth, but even after that is over He will continue to reign as king instead of the Father? (Since they must say that Christ reigns only for 1000 years, you will need to follow up with another question.)

Question #2: Since the Bible says (at Isaiah 9:7) that there will be no end to the reign of Christ, and the Watchtower says that it will last for only 1000 years, then in what sense will Christ reign as king forever? It is impossible for two kings to reign together!

• On page 68, paragraph 28, line 5, it says, "To prove worthy of protection during this coming destruction, we must exercise faith in Jesus Christ. (John 3:36) We must become his disciples and submit ourselves to him as our heavenly king. Will you do that?"

Question #1: What is the difference between the faith that Jehovah's Witnesses exercise in Jesus Christ and the faith exercised by millions of Bible-believing followers of Christ the world over? I believe that Jesus Christ existed before He came to this earth. I believe that He lived a perfect life upon this earth. I further believe that He died and shed His blood for all my personal sins. I have confessed that I am an ungodly sinner before God, and I have repented of my sins. I have exercised faith in the Lord Jesus Christ and asked Him to come into my innermost heart and be my personal Savior. What is wrong with this kind of faith?

Question #2: I have a question concerning John 3:36, which has been given here as a reference. This verse says, "He that believeth on the Son hath everlasting life: and he that believeth not the Son shall not see life; but the wrath of God abideth on him." I note that those who exercise true faith in the Lord Jesus Christ have been given "eternal life." It is something which they receive at the very time they put their faith in Christ. Do you, as a Jehovah's Witness, know that you have eternal life right now in the way this verse promises it? (If they are honest with you, they must say "No," because they believe that eternal life is something which will be given only after the thousand-year reign of

Christ to those who prove to be worthy and faithful.)

Question #3: If it is really true that a person will not possess everlasting life until after the millennial reign of Christ, then why doesn't the Bible have the verb "hath" in the future tense instead of the present tense?

Question #4: What does it mean that "the wrath of God abideth" on the person who does not exercise faith in the Lord Jesus Christ as his or her personal Savior?

Chapters 7 and 8
WHY ARE WE HERE? and WHAT HAPPENS AT DEATH?

I am combining these two chapters here because I have taken questions from both chapters. Chapter Seven shows that God created man and that he did not evolve by the process of evolution. In this chapter, however, the writers clearly deny the existence of an immaterial soul. Chapter Eight explains their view on death. They believe that men are annihilated at the time of death and enter a state of unconsciousness. To try to prove their false assumption they have to get rid of the soul, which they have tried to do in Chapter Seven, and redefine what the spirit is in Chapter Eight. The Watchtower's false teaching that "hell" is "man's common grave" is the foundation upon which all this misinterpretation is built. Since the foundation is false, then all the related doctrines are also.

• On page 73, paragraph 11, line 1, it says, "Since the human soul is man himself, then it cannot be some shadowy thing that lives inside the body or that can leave the body. Simply put, the Bible teaches that your soul is you." On page 77, paragraph 4, line 6, it says, "At death man's spirit, his life force, which is sustained by breathing, 'goes out.' It no longer exists. So man's senses of hearing, sight, touch, smell and taste, which depend upon his being able to think, all stop working. According to the Bible, the dead enter a state of complete unconsciousness." (They have stated it a little clearer in a previous book, *The Truth that Leads to Eternal Life*, on page 39, paragraph 13, line 1: "Whereas the human soul is the living person himself, the spirit is simply the life force that enables that person to be alive. The spirit lacks personality, nor can it do the things a person can do. It cannot think, speak, hear, see or feel.")

Question #1: If I understand the Watchtower's teaching correctly, they believe that only 144,000 people will go to heaven to live and reign with Christ. Is this correct?

Question #2: Is it also true that the Watchtower teaches that in 1914 all the members of the 144,000 up to that time were "resurrected" (raised as spirit beings) and went to heaven? (They should be familiar with this teaching, but some might not be.)

Question #3: Do they further teach that since that time, whenever members of the 144,000 die they go directly to heaven?

Question #4: Is it also correct that the Watchtower teaches that physical bodies cannot enter heaven and those people who go there are "spirit persons"?

Question #5: I have a real problem with this. If man is made up of only body and spirit, and the body goes into the grave and the spirit is only the life force, then this leaves nothing to go to heaven. So how can the Watchtower teach that those who go to heaven are "spirit beings" when no such thing exists—because they teach that the spirit of a man is simply the force that keeps the man alive? Since the personality, mind and will reside in the body, which lies in the grave, then these "spirit beings" could not be former human beings. (I don't think you will receive much of an answer.)

Question #6: I have thought long and hard about this impossible situation. There is only one way that I know by which the problem might be resolved. Let me speculate. The New World Translation says in 1 Corinthians 15:20, "However, now Christ has been raised up from the dead, the first fruits of those who have fallen asleep [in death]." Since Christ was the "first fruits," then those afterward would have to be in the pattern of Christ. Agreed? The 144,000 would have had to exist as angels before coming to this world. Then when they were on earth, they were humans. At the time of their death, they then cease to be humans anymore and are recreated as angels—in the form they were before becoming humans. So now they are back in the other world as "spirits" with "spirit bodies." Would you say that this is a possibility? (I do not believe any such thing, but am trying to get them to think. Since this is a new idea to them they are not likely to give you an answer, though they possibly will say "Yes" to get out of the pinch.)

Question #7: I do not want to get into a discussion on the soul, but there is one question I have. As we read before (page 73, paragraph 11, line 1), the Society teaches, "Since the human soul is man himself, then it cannot be some shadowy thing that lives inside the body or that can leave the body." Yet the Bible teaches that the soul *can* leave the body. Would you mind opening your NWT Bible to 1 Kings 17:21–22 and read these verses: "And he [Elijah] proceeded to stretch himself on the child three times and call to Jehovah and say: 'O Jehovah, my God, please, cause the soul of this child to come back within him.' Finally Jehovah listened to Elijah's voice, so that the soul of the child came back within him and he came to life." These verses clearly teach that the soul is something that can and did leave the body. Of course, when the soul came back into the child, the child became alive. Why does the Watchtower teach something different from what the Bible teaches? (Don't let them take you to other verses, but have them give you an answer about this verse. They might try to say it really means "spirit," but that is not what the Bible says—not even in their own translation.)

I cannot go through the whole book, but this will give you an idea of the kind of questions you can ask. If you would like to have more questions, you may write to me and order the questions for the complete book. See Appendix III for details.

APPENDIX II

BASIC CHRISTIAN DOCTRINES EXPLAINED

The Jehovah's Witnesses deny most of the basic doctrines of Christianity, yet they claim that they are the only group that is truly Christian. The Watchtower Society says that other groups are pagan and are of the devil.

The Society uses the Bible to try to prove its teachings. However, they take most passages out of context. Almost any teaching can be proven with verses or portions of verses taken out of context. Someone might say the Bible teaches that "there is no God." However, the entire sentence says, "The fool hath said in his heart, There is no God" (Ps. 14:1a).

Do not be deceived into thinking that the Witnesses know their Bible. They are only familiar with a few verses. The leaders redefine the Bible to make it say what they want it to say. We have looked at some of the ways that they do this.

Most Witnesses are well versed when it comes to attacking the doctrines of Christianity. However, they have been taught not to think on their own. They quote the verses the Society teaches them. They do not explore the Bible for themselves. Because of this, you must first get them to question what the Society has taught them before you can begin to explain what the Bible says.

In this chapter, I will explain the Trinity, the personality of the Holy Spirit, the immortality of the soul, the 144,000, and the future home of the Christian.

THE TRINITY

The doctrine of the Trinity is one of the hardest for a

231

Witness to accept. They have been taught that this is a pagan doctrine. Ask the Witness to refrain from calling the doctrine of the Trinity pagan until they prove to you that it is truly pagan. Ask them to produce a book or writing done by a "pagan"—a genuine pagan—whose view of the Trinity agrees with that taught by Bible-believing Christians. They cannot do this, but it will make them think.

Some of the most obvious proofs of the Trinity are:

The Bible teaches that there is only one God. The Watchtower Society teaches that Jesus is "a god" distinct and separate from the Father. They say that the the Father created the Son. This is in clear violation of the Bible. To teach that there is more than one God is a pagan doctrine called "polytheism." (See Deut. 4:35; 6:4; Isa. 43:10–11; 44:6, 8; 45:5, 14, 18, 21, 22; 46:9; Eph. 4:6; James 2:19; Jude 24–25.)

The Bible forbids man to worship any deity except God. Exodus 20:1–5 and Deuteronomy 5:6–9 both state this very clearly. In Isaiah 45:23 God says, "Unto me every knee shall bow." Then in Philippians 2:10 He says, "at the name of *Jesus* every knee shall bow" [Emphasis mine]. If every knee shall bow and if Jesus is not God, then the Father would be commanding people to break the law. He would never do that.

Hebrews 1:6 tells us that when Jesus was a baby, the angels worshiped Him. Men also worshiped the baby Jesus. The Witnesses try to get around this by saying that Jesus is given obeisance as "God's representative." But when pagans bow down to a stone or a wooden god, they also say that they are not bowing to the idol but to the god represented by the idol.

Wherever the Bible says Jesus was worshiped, the Society has changed the word "worship" to "obeisance." However, the Greek uses the same word for worship and obeisance. God forbids man to worship or bow down to anyone other than Himself. Since God commands man to worship Jesus, then Jesus Christ has to be God.

Jesus acknowledged as God. In Acts 10:25–26 and

Revelation 22:8–9, Peter and the angels refused the worship of men. However, when Thomas worshiped Jesus (John 20:28), Jesus commended Thomas. See also Hebrews 1:8.

Deuteronomy 10:17, Revelation 17:14, and Revelation 19:11–16 all mention the Lord of lords. The Revelation passages are speaking of Jesus Christ. Zechariah 14:9, 17 refers to the millennial kingdom when Jesus Christ is the ruler. All people will have to worship the King who is Jesus Christ.

One of the best verses to use with the Jehovah's Witnesses is Isaiah 9:6, which says, "For unto us a child is born, unto us a son is given: and the government shall be upon his shoulder: and his name shall be called Wonderful, Counsellor, The mighty God, The everlasting Father [literally, "the Father of eternity"], The Prince of Peace."

This verse refers to Jesus Christ. Ask the Witness to explain how Jesus became "the everlasting Father." Where in the Bible does it say that Jesus became a Father by having a literal son? Where does it say that God became a grandfather when Jesus had His Son? The Witness will not have any answer for these questions. Tell him that you will discuss the Trinity further after he answers those questions.

Other references that prove that Jesus is God are: Isaiah 41:4, 44:6, and 48:12 coupled with Revelation 1:11, 1:17, and 22:13. Jehovah God is called "the first and the last" or "the Alpha and the Omega." Jesus is also called "the Alpha and the Omega." Therefore, Jesus must be God.

John 5:23 tells us that all men are to honor the Son in the same way that they honor the Father. In John 10:28, Jesus says that He gives eternal life. In order to give eternal life, He must first possess eternal life. See also John 14:6, 17:2, and 20:31.

THE HOLY SPIRIT

The Jehovah's Witnesses deny the personality of the Holy Spirit. In the book *You Can Live Forever in Paradise on Earth* they write: "His holy spirit, which is his invisible active force, can be felt everywhere, over all the universe. By means of his holy spirit God created the heavens, the earth and all living things. . . . He can send out his spirit, his active force, to do whatever he wants even though he is far away" (p. 37). I once asked a Jehovah's Witness how God could tell something that is not a person how to create this universe and do His bidding? I did not get an answer.

In one of their major arguments, they say that the Holy Spirit cannot be a person because He can be "poured out." Acts 10:45 says, "And they of the circumcision which believed were astonished, as many as came with Peter, because that on the Gentiles also was *poured out* the gift of the Holy Ghost" [emphasis mine]. However, according to Watchtower teaching, man does not have a soul; he is a soul. They say that the human *soul* equals the human *body* plus the breath of life. Keep this in mind as we look at the following verses.

• First Samuel 1:15—Hannah said that she had "poured out my soul before the LORD."

• Job 10:10— "Hast thou not poured me out as milk?"

• Job 30:16—"And now my soul is poured out upon me."

• Isaiah 53:12—". . . he hath poured out his soul unto death."

To be consistent with their teaching that anything that can be poured out cannot be a person, they would have to say that a human being is not a person. Their argument that the Holy Spirit is not a person because He can be poured out is not biblical. (And it does not mesh with the Society's other teachings.)

The following verses show that the Holy Spirit is a person and is the third person of the Trinity.

• Acts 5:2–5—Peter calls the Holy Spirit "God" and says that He can be lied to.

• Matthew 29:19; 2 Corinthians 13:14—The divine formula: God the Father, God the Son, and God the Holy Spirit.

• John 14:26; 1 Corinthians 2:13; 1 John 2:27—The Holy Spirit teaches believers.

• John 14:16–26—Jesus tells His disciples that the Holy Spirit will be their Comforter and Helper when He returns to heaven.

• John 15:26–27—The Holy Spirit bears witness.

• Matthew 12:31–32—The Holy Spirit can be blasphemed.

• Acts 8:29—The Holy Spirit spoke to Philip and directed his ministry to the Ethiopian eunuch.

• Acts 16:6–7—The Holy Spirit forbade Paul to preach in the province of Asia.

• Romans 8:9; 1 Corinthians 3:16; 6:19—The Holy Spirit dwells in believers.

• Romans 8:26. The Holy Spirit makes intercession for us.

• Romans 15:16; 1 Peter 1:2—The Holy Spirit sanctifies the believer.

• Second Corinthians 13:14; Philippians 2:1—Believers can have fellowship or communion with the Holy Spirit.

THE IMMORTAL SOUL

The Jehovah's Witnesses say that man's soul is not separate from his body and it cannot live independently after death. The Bible tells us that the soul is distinct from the body. It teaches that the soul leaves the body at the time of death. It is not annihilated as the Witnesses claim.

• Genesis 35:18–19—Talks about Rachel's death. It says, "And the result was that as her soul was going out (because she died) . . ." (NWT). Her soul could not have gone out from her body if her soul was her body.

• First Kings 17:21–22—Probably one of the clearest passages in the Bible dealing with the soul and body. When the child's soul re-entered his body following Elijah's prayer, the child revived. The Watchtower Society's translation of these verses says, "O Jehovah, my God, please cause the soul of this child to come back within him. Finally Jehovah listened to Elijah's voice, so that the soul of the child came back within him and he came to life" (NWT). Even *their* translation contradicts their teachings!

• Matthew 10:28—Presents Jesus' teaching that the body can be killed while the soul remains alive. Jesus also taught that the soul could go to a place of suffering.

• First Thessalonians 5:23—Man has a body, a soul, and a spirit.

• Revelation 6:9–11—The body was slain, but the soul was alive and conscious.

THE 144,000

The Watchtower Society and some other cults teach that only 144,000 individuals will go to heaven. The Bible tells us that heaven is open to all those who put their faith and trust in the Lord Jesus Christ as their personal Savior.

The Watchtower Society took the number 144,000 from Revelation 7:4 and Revelation 14:1. The Witnesses do not take most of the Bible literally, but they do certainly take these verses literally. However, they ignore the surrounding verses.

Since the Watchtower Society makes the number 144,000 literal, they also should make the number in Revelation 7:9 literal, where it says, "After this I beheld, and, lo, a great multitude, which no man could number, of all nations, and kindreds, and people, and tongues, stood before the throne, and before the Lamb, clothed with white robes, and palms in their hands." And where is God's throne? Verses 11 through 17 make it plain: heaven. But J.W.'s don't believe in a great heavenly crowd which no man can number. The Society teaches that the great crowd is those who make up the bulk of the four-and-one-half million Jehovah's Witnesses today who will *remain on earth.*

The Bible is clear that the number going to heaven is not restricted to 144,000. But even if it were true that only 144,000 go to heaven, the Bible never says specifically that they are the ones who live and reign with Christ like the Watchtower Society claims. In the Book of Revelation we are given two qualifications for living and reigning with Christ for 1000 years. Namely, (1) Faithfulness unto death, (2) Participation in the first resurrection.

Revelation 20:4 reads: "And I saw thrones, and they sat upon them, and judgment was given unto them: and I saw the souls of them that were beheaded for the witness of Jesus, and for the word of God, and which had not worshipped the beast, neither his image, neither had received his mark upon their forehead, or in their hands; and they lived and reigned with Christ a thousand years." Revelation 20:6 reads: "Blessed and holy is he that hath part in the first resurrection: on such the second death hath no power, but they shall be priests of God and of Christ, and shall reign with him a thousand years."

THE FUTURE HOME OF THE CHRISTIAN

The Society has taught since 1935 that its followers will not go to heaven but will go to the new earth. Before 1935 it taught that its followers would make up the 144,000 who would go to heaven. However, the Society changed its teaching when it decided the quota of 144,000 was full. The verses they use are:

  • Psalm 37:9—"For evildoers shall be cut off: but those that wait upon the LORD, they shall inherit the earth."

  • Psalm 37:11—"But the meek shall inherit the earth; and shall delight themselves in the abundance of peace."

  • Psalm 37:29—"The righteous shall inherit the land, and dwell therein for ever."

(But these verses, when read in context, refer to the Jewish people.)

  • Matthew 5:5—"Blessed are the meek: for they shall inherit the earth."

Of course, they ignore Matthew 5:3, which says, "Blessed are the poor in spirit: for theirs is the kingdom of heaven," and Matthew 5:10 which says, "Blessed are they which are persecuted for righteousness' sake: for theirs is the kingdom of heaven." It is strange that they claim they are being persecuted; yet they do not want to go to heaven!

One of the questions I ask a Witness is: "If living on the new earth is taught in the Bible and life there is supposed to be so wonderful, why did the Society not teach this during its first fifty-five years? Why did they wait until the 144,000 quota was full before teaching about the new earth?"

I have never received a reasonable answer to this question. And I cannot understand why anyone would want to labor to clean up a destroyed earth when they could go to a perfect heaven created by God.

The following verses tell us that heaven is the home of the Christian: Matthew 5:3,10; John 14:1–3, 17:24; 2 Corinthians 5:1–4; Philippians 3:20; 1 Thessalonians 4:17; 2 Thessalonians 2:1; 2 Timothy 4:18; Hebrews 11:16 (the Jehovah's Witnesses, however, teach that the Old Testament saints mentioned in this chapter will not go to heaven); and 1 Peter 1:4.

APPENDIX III

SOURCE MATERIAL REFERENCE

The following are good sources for obtaining additional material on the Jehovah's Witnesses:

1. Comments from the Friends, P.O. Box 840, Stoughton, MA 02072. They issue a helpful pamphlet about four times a year, edited by David Reed, a former J.W. He has several good books that may be ordered at the above address or obtained through your local Christian bookstore.

Behind the Watchtower Curtain by David Reed (Crowne Publications, 1989).

Crisis of Conscience by Raymond Franz, a former J.W. governing body member and a nephew of the late president of the Watchtower, Fred Franz.

How to Rescue Your Loved One from the Watchtower by David Reed (Baker Book House, 1989).

2. Free Minds, Inc., P.O. Box 3818, Manhattan Beach, CA 90266. They produce a helpful publication bimonthly. It is edited by Randall Watters, a former J.W. Some of his publications are:

Refuting Jehovah's Witnesses and *Defending the Faith* by Randall Watters. (These come as a pair.)

Thus Saith . . . the Governing Body of Jehovah's Witnesses by Randall Watters.

3. Witness Inc., P.O. Box 597, Clayton, CA 94517. Duane Magnani, the founder, is a former J.W.

The Watchtower Files by Duane Magnani (Bethany House Publications).

Who is the Faithful & Wise Servant? by Duane Magnani.

4. Love to Share Ministries, 345 George Dye Road, Trenton, NJ 08691. Rev. Wilbur Lingle. I have compiled into packets a lot of pages containing the old Watchtower false prophecies and doctrinal changes, so that they can be used in witnessing. These are photocopies of their own material. They are on individual sheets, so they can be shown to a Jehovah's Witness very easily. (Much of this material can be found in books, but a Jehovah's Witness will not look at anything found in a book, even if it is taken from their own writings.) I also have a complete set of questions for the section started in Appendix I, on how to witness from the Watchtower book *You Can Live Forever in Paradise on Earth.*

If you have any questions once you have begun to witness to a Jehovah's Witness, feel free to call me at (609) 890-8751 for help and encouragement. I also conduct seminars based on this book. Please contact me.

The insert which follows is intended as a working tool for your use when actively seeking to approach Jehovah's Witnesses.

In order that it may be used as such, the publisher gladly grants the purchaser the right to make one or more photocopies of this insert for his or her personal use, *free of charge.*

All other copyright restrictions apply.

This book was produced by the Christian Literature Crusade. We hope it has been helpful to you in living the Christian life. CLC is a literature mission with ministry in over 45 countries worldwide. If you would like to know more about us, or are interested in opportunities to serve with a faith mission, we invite you to write to:

Christian Literature Crusade
P.O.Box 1449
Fort Washington, PA 19034